PENGUIN POPULAR CLASSICS

ROMEO AND JULIET
BY WILLIAM SHAKESPEARE

Aran uthayakumar

PENGUIN POPULAR CLASSICS

ROMEO AND JULIET

WILLIAM SHAKESPEARE

PENGUIN BOOKS

PENGUIN BOOKS

Published by the Penguin Group
Penguin Books Ltd, 80 Strand, London WC2R 0RL, England
Penguin Putnam Inc., 375 Hudson Street, New York, New York 10014, USA
Penguin Books Australia Ltd, Ringwood, Victoria, Australia
Penguin Books Canada Ltd, 10 Alcorn Avenue, Toronto, Ontario, Canada M4V 3B2
Penguin Books India (P) Ltd, 11 Community Centre, Panchsheel Park,
New Delhi — 110 017, India
Penguin Books (NZ) Ltd, Cnr Rosedale and Airborne Roads, Albany, Auckland,
New Zealand
Penguin Books (South Africa) (Pty) Ltd, 24 Sturdee Avenue, Rosebank 2196, South Africa

Penguin Books Ltd, Registered Offices: 80 Strand, London WC2R 0RL, England

www.penguin.com

Published in Penguin Popular Classics 1994
010

Editorial matter copyright © G. B. Harrison, 1937

Printed in Great Britain by Clays Ltd, St Ives plc

ISBN-13: 978-0-14062-338-3

www.greenpenguin.co.uk

MIX
Paper from
responsible sources
FSC® C018179

Penguin Books is committed to a sustainable
future for our business, our readers and our planet.
This book is made from Forest Stewardship
Council™ certified paper.

ALWAYS LEARNING   **PEARSON**

CONTENTS

THE WORKS OF SHAKESPEARE

WILLIAM SHAKESPEARE

William Shakespeare was born at Stratford upon Avon in April, 1564. He was the third child, and eldest son, of John Shakespeare and Mary Arden. His father was one of the most prosperous men of Stratford, who held in turn the chief offices in the town. His mother was of gentle birth, the daughter of Robert Arden of Wilmcote. In December, 1582, Shakespeare married Ann Hathaway, daughter of a farmer of Shottery, near Stratford; their first child Susanna was baptized on May 6, 1583, and twins, Hamnet and Judith, on February 22, 1585. Little is known of Shakespeare's early life; but it is unlikely that a writer who dramatized such an incomparable range and variety of human kinds and experiences should have spent his early manhood entirely in placid pursuits in a country town. There is one tradition, not universally accepted, that he fled from Stratford because he was in trouble for deer stealing, and had fallen foul of Sir Thomas Lucy, the local magnate; another that he was for some time a schoolmaster.

From 1592 onwards the records are much fuller. In March, 1592, the Lord Strange's players produced a new play at the Rose Theatre called *Harry the Sixth*, which was very successful, and was probably the *First Part of Henry VI*. In the autumn of 1592 Robert Greene, the best known of the professional writers, as he was dying wrote a letter to three fellow writers in which he warned them against the ingratitude of players in general, and in particular against an 'upstart crow' who 'supposes he is as much able to bombast out a blank verse as the best of you: and being an absolute Johannes Factotum is in his own conceit the only

Shake-scene in a country.' This is the first reference to Shakespeare, and the whole passage suggests that Shakespeare had become suddenly famous as a playwright. At this time Shakespeare was brought into touch with Edward Alleyne the great tragedian, and Christopher Marlowe, whose thundering parts of Tamburlaine, the Jew of Malta, and Dr Faustus Alleyne was acting, as well as Hieronimo, the hero of Kyd's *Spanish Tragedy*, the most famous of all Elizabethan plays.

In April, 1593, Shakespeare published his poem *Venus and Adonis*, which was dedicated to the young Earl of Southampton: it was a great and lasting success, and was reprinted nine times in the next few years. In May, 1594, his second poem, *The Rape of Lucrece*, was also dedicated to Southampton.

There was little playing in 1593, for the theatres were shut during a severe outbreak of the plague; but in the autumn of 1594, when the plague ceased, the playing companies were reorganized, and Shakespeare became a sharer in the Lord Chamberlain's company who went to play in the Theatre in Shoreditch. During these months Marlowe and Kyd had died. Shakespeare was thus for a time without a rival. He had already written the three parts of *Henry VI*, *Richard III*, *Titus Andronicus*, *The Two Gentlemen of Verona*, *Love's Labour's Lost*, *The Comedy of Errors*, and *The Taming of the Shrew*. Soon afterwards he wrote the first of his greater plays – *Romeo and Juliet* – and he followed this success in the next three years with *A Midsummer Night's Dream*, *Richard II*, and *The Merchant of Venice*. The two parts of *Henry VI*, introducing Falstaff, the most popular of all his comic characters, were written in 1597–8.

The company left the Theatre in 1597 owing to disputes

over a renewal of the ground lease, and went to play at the Curtain in the same neighbourhood. The disputes continued throughout 1598, and at Christmas the players settled the matter by demolishing the old Theatre and re-erecting a new playhouse on the South bank of the Thames, near Southwark Cathedral. This playhouse was named the Globe. The expenses of the new building were shared by the chief members of the Company, including Shakespeare, who was now a man of some means. In 1596 he had bought New Place, a large house in the centre of Stratford, for £60, and through his father purchased a coat-of-arms from the Heralds, which was the official recognition that he and his family were gentlefolk.

By the summer of 1598 Shakespeare was recognized as the greatest of English dramatists. Booksellers were printing his more popular plays, at times even in pirated or stolen versions, and he received a remarkable tribute from a young writer named Francis Meres, in his book *Palladis Tamia*. In a long catalogue of English authors Meres gave Shakespeare more prominence than any other writer, and mentioned by name twelve of his plays.

Shortly before the Globe was opened, Shakespeare had completed the cycle of plays dealing with the whole story of the Wars of the Roses with *Henry V*. It was followed by *As You Like it*, and *Julius Cæsar*, the first of the maturer tragedies. In the next three years he wrote *Troilus and Cressida*, *The Merry Wives of Windsor*, *Hamlet*, and *Twelfth Night*.

On March 24, 1603, Queen Elizabeth died. The company had often performed before her, but they found her successor a far more enthusiastic patron. One of the first acts of King James was to take over the company and to promote them to be his own servants, so that henceforward they were known as the King's Men. They acted now very frequently at Court, and prospered accordingly. In the early years of the reign Shakespeare wrote the more sombre comedies, *All's Well that Ends Well*, and *Measure for Measure*, which were followed by *Othello*, *Macbeth*, and *King Lear*. Then he returned to Roman themes with *Antony and Cleopatra* and *Coriolanus*.

Since 1601 Shakespeare had been writing less, and there were now a number of rival dramatists who were introducing new styles of drama, particularly Ben Jonson (whose first successful comedy, *Every Man in his Humour*, was acted by Shakespeare's company in 1598), Chapman, Dekker, Marston, and Beaumont and Fletcher who began to write in 1607. In 1608 the King's Men acquired a second playhouse, an indoor private theatre in the fashionable quarter of the Blackfriars. At private theatres, plays were performed indoors; the prices charged were higher than in the public playhouses, and the audience consequently was more select. Shakespeare seems to have retired from the stage about this time: his name does not occur in the various lists of players after 1607. Henceforward he lived for the most part at Stratford, where he was regarded as one of the most important citizens. He still wrote a few plays, and he tried his hand at the new form of tragi-comedy – a play with tragic incidents but a happy ending – which Beaumont and Fletcher had popularized. He wrote four of these – *Pericles, Cymbeline, The Winter's Tale*, and *The Tempest*, which was acted at Court in 1611. For the last four years of his life he lived in retirement. His son Hamnet had died in 1596: his two daughters were now married. Shakespeare died at Stratford upon Avon on April 23, 1616, and was buried in the chancel of the church, before the high altar. Shortly afterwards a memorial which still exists, with a portrait bust, was set up on the North wall. His wife survived him.

When Shakespeare died fourteen of his plays had been separately published in Quarto booklets. In 1623 his surviving fellow actors, John Heming and Henry Condell, with the co-operation of a number of printers, published a collected edition of thirty-six plays in one Folio volume, with an engraved portrait, memorial verses by Ben Jonson and others, and an Epistle to the Reader in which Heming and Condell make the interesting note that Shakespeare's 'hand and mind went together, and what he thought, he uttered with that easiness that we have scarce received from him a blot in his papers.'

The plays as printed in the Quartos or the Folio differ considerably from the usual modern text. They are often not divided into scenes, and sometimes not even into acts. Nor are there place-headings at the beginning of each scene, because in the Elizabethan theatre there was no scenery. They are carelessly printed and the spelling is erratic.

THE ELIZABETHAN THEATRE

Although plays of one sort and another had been acted for many generations, no permanent playhouse was erected in England until 1576. In the 1570's the Lord Mayor and Aldermen of the City of London and the players were constantly at variance. As a result James Burbage, then the leader of the great Earl of Leicester's players, decided that he would erect a playhouse outside the jurisdiction of the

Lord Mayor, where the players would no longer be hindered by the authorities. Accordingly in 1576 he built the Theatre in Shoreditch, at that time a suburb of London. The experiment was successful, and by 1592 there were two more playhouses in London, the Curtain (also in Shoreditch), and the Rose on the south bank of the river, near Southwark Cathedral.

Elizabethan players were accustomed to act on a variety of stages; in the great hall of a nobleman's house, or one of the Queen's palaces, in town halls and in yards, as well as their own theatre.

The public playhouse for which most of Shakespeare's plays were written was a small and intimate affair. The outside measurement of the Fortune Theatre, which was built in 1600 to rival the new Globe, was but eighty feet square. Playhouses were usually circular or hexagonal, with three tiers of galleries looking down upon the yard or pit, which was open to the sky. The stage jutted out into the yard so that the actors came forward into the midst of their audience.

Over the stage there was a roof, and on either side doors by which the characters entered or disappeared. Over the back of the stage ran a gallery or upper stage which was used whenever an upper scene was needed, as when Romeo climbs up to Juliet's bedroom, or the citizens of Angiers address King John from the walls. The space beneath this upper stage was known as the tiring house; it was concealed from the audience by a curtain which would be drawn back to reveal an inner stage, for such scenes as the witches' cave in Macbeth, Prospero's cell, or Juliet's tomb.

There was no general curtain concealing the whole stage, so that all scenes on the main stage began with an entrance

THE GLOBE THEATRE
Wood-engraving by R. J. Beedham after a reconstruction by J. C. Adams

and ended with an exit. Thus in tragedies the dead must be carried away. There was no scenery, and therefore no limit to the number of scenes, for a scene came to an end when the characters left the stage. When it was necessary for the exact locality of a scene to be known, then Shakespeare indicated it in the dialogue; otherwise a simple property or a garment was sufficient; a chair or stool showed an indoor scene, a man wearing riding boots was a messenger, a king wearing armour was on the battlefield, or the like. Such simplicity was on the whole an advantage; the spectator was not distracted by the setting and Shakespeare was able to use as many scenes as he wished. The action passed by very quickly: a play of 2500 lines of verse could be acted in two hours. Moreover, since the actor was so close to his audience, the slightest subtlety of voice and gesture was easily appreciated.

The company was a 'Fellowship of Players', who were all partners and sharers. There were usually ten to fifteen full members, with three or four boys, and some paid servants. Shakespeare had therefore to write for his team. The chief actor in the company was Richard Burbage, who first distinguished himself as Richard III; for him Shakespeare wrote his great tragic parts. An important member of the company was the clown or low comedian. From 1594 to 1600 the company's clown was Will Kemp; he was succeeded by Robert Armin. No women were allowed to appear on the stage, and all women's parts were taken by boys.

ROMEO AND JULIET

The tragedy of *Romeo and Juliet* was first produced about 1595, and was thus one of the plays which the Lord Chamberlain's Company performed during their occupation of the Theatre in Shoreditch. From the first it was popular. It was written at a time when the brief vogue for sonnet-writing was at its height, and it fitted perfectly with the general mood of those poets who were exploring and expressing the sensations of love during the early 1590's.

The story, in one form or another, was often told in the fifteenth and sixteenth centuries, but Shakespeare's source was an English poem published in 1562, called *The Tragical History of Romeus and Juliet*, by Arthur Brooke, who noted in the preface that he had lately seen the story dramatized. Brooke's verse was tedious, but the poem was a useful foundation, for he gave many hints for the principal characters, including a Nurse garrulously reminiscent of Juliet's infancy:

A pretty babe (quoth she) it was when it was yong:
Lord, how it could full prettily have prated with it tong.

Shakespeare followed Brooke closely, but made some important changes, particularly in the speed of the tragedy. In Brooke's story the events covered two months; in the play beginning and ending occur within five days. Brooke's verse was hardly suitable for the dialogue, but occasionally he was able to provide lines which Shakespeare transmuted. Juliet's thoughts before she drank the Friar's potion (p. 115, l. 12 – p. 116, l. 23) were thus described by Brooke:

What do I know (quoth she) if that this powder shall
Sooner or later than it should or else not work at all?
And then my craft descried as open as the day,
The people's tale and laughing stock shall I remain for aye.
And what know I (quoth she) if serpents odious,
And other beasts and worms that are of nature veno-
    mous,
That wonted are to lurk in dark caves under ground,
And commonly, as I have heard, in dead men's tombs
    are found,
Shall harm me, yea or nay, where I shall lie as dead? –
Or how shall I that alway have in so fresh air been bred,
Endure the loathsome stink of such an heaped store
Of carcases, not yet consum'd, and bones that long
    before
Intombed were, where I my sleeping place shall have,
Where all my ancestors do rest, my kindred's common
    grave?
Shall not the friar and my Romeus, when they come,
Find me (if I awake before) y-stifled in the tomb?
And whilst she in these thoughts doth dwell somewhat
    too long,
The force of her imagining anon did wax so strong,
That she surmised she saw, out of the hollow vault,
(A grizzly thing to look upon) the carcase of Tybalt;
Right in the selfsame sort that she few days before
Had seen him in his blood embru'd, to death eke
    wounded sore.
And then when she again within herself had weigh'd
That quick she should be buried there, and by his side
    be laid,
All comfortless, for she shall living fere have none,

But many a rotten carcase, and full many a naked bone;
Her dainty tender parts gan shiver all for dread,
Her golden hairs did stand upright upon her childish
    head.
Then pressed with the fear that she there lived in,
A sweat as cold as mountain ice pierc'd through her
    tender skin,
That with the moisture hath wet every part of hers:
And more besides, she vainly thinks whilst vainly thus
    she fears,
A thousand bodies dead have compassed her about,
And lest they will dismember her she greatly stands in
    doubt.
But when she felt her strength began to wear away,
By little and little, and in her heart her fear increased
    aye,
Dreading that weakness might, or foolish cowardise,
Hinder the execution of the purpos'd enterprise,
As she had frantic been, in haste the glass she cought,
And up she drank the mixture quite, withouten farther
    thought.
Then on her breast she cross'd her armes long and
    small
And so, her senses failing her, into a trance did fall.

The play was first published in a quarto early in 1597,
with the title page '*An Excellent conceited Tragedie of Romeo
and Juliet. As it hath been often (with great applause) plaid
publiquely, by the right Honourable the L. of Hunsdon his Servants*'. The players were known as Lord Hunsdon's between
July 1596, and March 1597. Their former patron, Henry
Carey, Lord Hunsdon, who was Lord Chamberlain, died

on 23rd July, 1596. His son George, Lord Hunsdon, then became their patron: he succeeded his father as Lord Chamberlain on 17th March, 1597. This edition is known as the First Quarto. It is one of several pirated editions of Shakespeare's plays which were not printed either from the author's manuscript or from a direct copy of it.

In 1599 a Second Quarto appeared, with the title-page: *The Most Excellent and lamentable Tragedie of Romeo and Juliet. Newly corrected, augmented, and amended: As it hath bene sundry times publiquely acted, by the right Honourable the Lord Chamberlaine his Servants.* This Quarto was reprinted in 1609 '*As it hath beene sundrie times publiquely Acted, by the Kings Maiesties Servants at the Globe. Newly corrected, augmented and amended.*' An undated quarto and a quarto of 1637 also exist. For the Folio of 1623 a copy of the Third Quarto was used by the printer.

The First Quarto is a puzzling production. Many passages which appear in the Second Quarto are roughly paraphrased; others are omitted. The Folio text contains about 3,000 lines, the First Quarto only some 2,300. In the early scenes it follows the good text fairly closely, but in the later the differences are considerable. Nevertheless, unlike the pirated quartos of *Hamlet*, *The Merry Wives of Windsor*, and *Henry V* the text as a whole is comparatively good; and it often gives readings by which the mistakes of the Second Quarto can be corrected. Perhaps it was the work of a reporter, but if so, he must have been helped either by someone who knew the play intimately or else had seen a playhouse copy of the script. Moreover, there are some striking similarities in the printing of the First and Second Quarto. The speeches of the Nurse, for instance, in Act I Scene 3 for some reason were printed in italic type in both editions. Apparently therefore the printer of the Second Quarto had a copy of the First Quarto by him. The First Quarto has also some vivid stage directions, which show how the play was acted.

The Second Quarto gives the full text of the play, and was probably set up from Shakespeare's manuscript. The text shows signs of revision and rewriting; these are indicated in the Notes. It is less carefully printed than the Folio, but is nearer to the original. In all these early texts, division into Acts and Scenes is lacking.

An editor of *Romeo and Juliet* has therefore many problems. Editors in the past have usually printed a text based on the Second Quarto, but using the First Quarto where its readings appeared preferable. In this edition the text follows the Second Quarto closely. A few necessary emendations, generally accepted by editors, have been made. The punctuation also follows the Second Quarto, but has been somewhat modified, usually with the aid of the Folio text. The Elizabethan practice was to punctuate a speech for delivery, and some of the punctuation in the Second Quarto is striking, but at times speeches are so lightly punctuated that the meaning is confused. Some of the stage directions peculiar to the First Quarto have been added: these are indicated by a pointed bracket ⟨ ⟩. The text as a whole may thus, at first sight, present some unfamiliarities to readers used to the 'accepted text', but it is nearer to that used in Shakespeare's own playhouse.

THE STAGING OF
ROMEO AND JULIET

The stage directions in the First and Second Quartos are so unusually full that it is possible to attempt a reconstruction of the action on the Elizabethan stage. In the following analysis of the production, which must naturally be conjectural in parts, the stage directions from the First Quarto are noted in *italics* and single quotation marks [' ']; and stage directions from the Second Quarto in *italics* and double quotation marks [" "]. In following the analysis the illustration on p. 13 should be used.

The parts of the stage mentioned are:

RIGHT and LEFT DOORS: the doors opening on to the main stage, right being the actor's right (and the spectator's left).

RECESS: the back of the stage, covered by curtains when not in use; in the illustration the curtains are shown *open*.

CHAMBER: the upper stage above the recess, covered by curtains when not in use; in the illustration the curtains over the CHAMBER are *closed*.

WINDOW: either right or left of the CHAMBER.

I:

The Chorus comes forward through the closed curtains of the RECESS to the front of the stage, says his lines, and goes back through the same curtains.

I, I:

"*Enter Sampson and Gregory with swords and bucklers of the House of Capulet,*" by the RIGHT door. At the LEFT door enter Abraham and Balthasar of the Montagues. Benvolio enters at the RIGHT door. Tybalt enters by the LEFT door. During the fight, "*enter three or four citizens with clubs or partisans,*" through the curtain of the RECESS. "*Enter old Capulet, in his gown, and his wife,*" by the RIGHT door. "*Enter old Montague and his wife,*" by the LEFT door. "*Enter Prince Escalus with his train,*" through the

RECESS. The Prince goes out through the RECESS. Capulet
and his party go out through the RIGHT door, leaving Montague, Lady Montague, and Benvolio. Romeo enters through the
RECESS curtains. Benvolio draws attention to his approach with
the phrase: "See where he comes! So please you, step aside."
(Some such phrase as "See where he comes" is the usual method
of drawing attention to a character who is entering from the
rear of the stage.) Montague and his wife go out by the LEFT
door; after some talk Benvolio and Romeo follow them.

I, 2:

Capulet and Count Paris, followed by Peter, enter by the RIGHT
door and go out again, leaving Peter. Benvolio and Romeo
enter by the LEFT door and read the letter. At the end of the
scene, Peter goes out RIGHT; Romeo and Benvolio go out
LEFT.

I, 3:

The curtains in the CHAMBER above are opened, revealing Lady
Capulet and Nurse. Juliet joins them. A servingman enters to
say that the guests have arrived. The curtains over the CHAMBER
are closed.

I, 4:

By the RIGHT door, "*enter Romeo and Mercutio, Benvolio and five
or six other Maskers, torchbearers.*" After a while, "*they march a-
bout the stage and Servingmen come forth with napkins*" through
the curtains of the RECESS. Romeo and party remain on the
stage, as

[I, 5:][1]

the curtains of the RECESS are opened and at the back of the
stage enter old Capulet with "*all the guests and gentlewomen to the
Maskers. Music plays and they dance.*" Tybalt goes out RIGHT. At
the end of the scene, Capulet's party goes out, on either side at
the back of the RECESS. The others go out by the RIGHT and
LEFT doors. The curtains of the RECESS are closed.

[1] The scenes in brackets [ ] have been created by editors; in the
original texts the action is not interrupted.

II:

The Chorus comes through the curtains of the RECESS, advances to the centre of the stage, delivers his lines, and goes back.

II, 1:

"*Enter Romeo alone*," by the LEFT door. He advances to the front of the stage and says:
>"Can I go forward when my heart is here?
>Turn back, dull earth, and find thy centre out."

As he moves toward the back of the stage, Benvolio and Mercutio enter by the LEFT door. Romeo hides by the right pillar (i.e., he keeps the pillar between himself and the other two). Benvolio and Mercutio go out LEFT.

[II, 2:]

When they have gone, Romeo is about to continue his move to the back when Juliet opens the WINDOW and looks out. Romeo pauses and then goes toward her. They converse. A voice calls for Juliet; she goes from the WINDOW, but quickly returns. The lovers bid good night. Juliet closes the WINDOW, and Romeo goes out RIGHT.

II, 3:

"*Enter Friar alone with a basket*," through the curtains of the RECESS; he comes forward. Romeo enters by the RIGHT door. They go in together through the curtains of the RECESS.

II, 4:

Benvolio and Mercutio enter by the LEFT door. Romeo enters through the curtains of the RECESS. "*Enter Nurse and her man*" by the RIGHT door. Benvolio and Mercutio go out by the LEFT door. After his conversation with the Nurse, Romeo goes out LEFT, and she goes out RIGHT.

II, 5:

The curtains in the CHAMBER above are opened, revealing Juliet. The Nurse enters. At the end of the scene the curtains of the CHAMBER are closed.

II, 6:

The curtains of the RECESS are opened revealing Friar Laurence and Romeo. The RECESS is now the Friar's cell. Through the door at the back of the RECESS '*enter Juliet, somewhat fast, and embraceth Romeo.*' As the Friar prepares to marry the lovers the curtains of the RECESS are closed.

III, 1:

"*Enter Mercutio, Benvolio and men,*" by the LEFT door. By the RIGHT door, enter Tybalt and others. Romeo enters through the RECESS curtains. Tybalt draws attention to his entry with "Here comes my man." Tybalt and Mercutio fight; '*Tybalt under Romeo's arm thrusts Mercutio in; and flies*' through the RIGHT door. The page goes out by the LEFT door. Mercutio, supported by Benvolio, goes out through the LEFT door, whence Benvolio emerges to say that Mercutio is dead. Tybalt re-enters by the RIGHT door. Romeo and Tybalt fight and Tybalt is slain. Romeo runs out by the LEFT door. The citizens enter through the curtains of the RECESS, followed by the Prince. Capulet and his wife enter by the RIGHT door. Montague and his wife enter by the LEFT. At the end of the scene, all go out by the ways in which they have entered, the body of Tybalt being carried out through the RIGHT door.

III, 2:

The curtains of the CHAMBER above are opened, revealing Juliet alone. '*Enter Nurse, wringing her hands, with the ladder of cords in her lap.*' At the end of the scene the curtains of the CHAMBER are closed.

III, 3:

The curtains of the RECESS are opened; the RECESS once more represents the Friar's cell. The Friar calls to Romeo, who comes in from the side. The Nurse knocks at the back of the door of the RECESS; she enters through the door at the back of the RECESS. At the end of the scene, the Nurse goes out by the door in the RECESS, and the curtains are closed.

III, 4:

Capulet, Lady Capulet, and Paris enter by the RIGHT door. Paris goes out by the RIGHT door as Capulet and Lady Capulet go in through the curtains of the RECESS.

III, 5:

The curtains of the CHAMBER above are opened. '*Enter Romeo and Juliet at the window.*' '*He goeth down*' by the ladder of cords and goes out LEFT. Juliet pulls up the ladder; '*she goeth down from the window.*' She shuts the WINDOW and passes into the CHAMBER as Lady Capulet enters. Capulet and the Nurse come to them and go out again. The Nurse goes out, leaving Juliet alone. The curtains of the CHAMBER are closed.

IV, 1:

The curtains of the RECESS are opened, disclosing Friar Laurence and Paris, as if in Friar Laurence's cell. Juliet enters by the door at the back of the RECESS. Paris goes out through the door at the back of the RECESS. The Friar closes the door at Juliet's words: "Oh, shut the door." At the end of the scene, the curtains are closed over the RECESS.

IV, 2:

"*Enter Father Capulet, Mother, Nurse and Servingmen, two or three,*" by the RIGHT door. The Servingmen go out RIGHT. Juliet enters through the curtains of the RECESS: "See where she comes from shrift with merry look." Juliet and the Nurse go out through the curtains of the RECESS. Capulet and his wife go out by the RIGHT door.

IV, 3:

The curtains of the CHAMBER above are opened, revealing Juliet and the Nurse laying clothes on the bed. Lady Capulet enters. She goes out with the Nurse. Juliet takes the potion; '*she falls upon her bed within the curtains.*' The curtains of the CHAMBER are closed.

IV, 4:

The curtains of the RECESS are opened; the inner stage has now become the hall of Capulet's house. Enter Lady Capulet and Nurse, '*with herbs.*' Capulet enters. Lady Capulet and the Nurse go out at the side of the RECESS. "*Enter three or four with spits and logs and baskets,*" who pass across the RECESS and go out. Capulet calls for the Nurse, who comes back. He tells her to make haste to call the bride. She goes up the STAIRS at the back of the RECESS.

[IV, 5:]

The Nurse from within opens the curtains of the CHAMBER. Juliet is revealed lying on her bed. The Nurse tries to awaken Juliet and at her cries Lady Capulet and then Capulet go up the STAIRS at the back of the RECESS and appear in the CHAMBER. The Friar and the Count enter the CHAMBER. After their lamentations, '*they all but the Nurse go forth, casting rosemary on her and shutting the curtains.*' In the act of closing the curtains of the CHAMBER, the Nurse is left standing on the BALCONY in front of the closed curtains. Musicians enter on the stage below. She looks down from the BALCONY and speaks to them and then she passes into the CHAMBER through the closed curtains. Peter enters at the back of the RECESS, and talks to the musicians, who go out by the RIGHT door. The curtains of the RECESS are closed.

V, I:

Romeo enters by the LEFT door. '*Enter Balthasar, his man, boot-ed*' – thereby indicating that he has come a long journey on horseback. Balthasar goes out by the LEFT door. Romeo goes over to the RIGHT door (which now becomes the entrance to the Apothecary's shop) and knocks. The Apothecary comes out; he delivers the poison to Romeo, goes back, and shuts the door. Romeo goes out by the LEFT door.

V, 2:

Friar John comes in by the RIGHT door as Friar Laurence enters through the curtains of the RECESS. Each goes out as he came in.

v, 3:

By the RIGHT door, 'enter County Paris and his Page with flowers and sweet water.' Paris goes up to the LEFT door (which now becomes the entrance to the burial vault of the Capulets). 'Paris strews the tomb with flowers.' The Page whistles. Paris dodges behind the left pillar to watch. By the RIGHT door, 'enter Romeo and Balthasar, with a torch, a mattock, and a crow of iron.' Romeo goes up to the LEFT door. His man Balthasar crosses the stage as if to go out by the RIGHT door, but comes back and hides by the right pillar. 'Romeo opens the tomb'; i.e., he puts his crowbar to the LEFT door and pries it open at the words "Thus I enforce thy rotten jaws to open." Paris steps forward. They fight. The Page runs out by the RIGHT door. As Paris dies, he says: "Open the tomb, lay me with Juliet." Romeo picks up the body, and at the words "I'll bury thee in a triumphant grave" passes through the open LEFT door. The curtains of the RECESS are opened, revealing Juliet lying on a bier, and the shrouded corpse of Tybalt. Romeo appears in the RECESS and lays Paris's body down. He takes the poison and falls dead. By the RIGHT door, "enter Friar with lanthorn, crow and spade." He crosses the stage. 'Friar stoops and looks on the blood and weapons.' He goes in through the open LEFT door and reappears in the RECESS as Juliet begins to stir. Friar Laurence comes forward and runs away by the RIGHT door. Juliet speaks to her dead lover and as the boy and the Watch come in through the RIGHT door she stabs herself.

By the RIGHT door then enter, in succession, Balthasar, Friar Laurence and Watchmen, the Prince, Capulet and his wife, Montague. They pass to the back of the stage and stand round the bodies in the RECESS.

The Prince then leads them forward and commands: "Seal up the mouth of outrage for a while." At these words, the curtains across the RECESS are closed, concealing the four bodies, and the LEFT door is also closed. After Friar Laurence's tale and the closing words of the Prince, all go out in procession by the RIGHT door.

The Most Excellent
and Lamentable Tragedy of
Romeo and Juliet

THE ACTORS' NAMES

ESCALES, prince of Verona

PARIS, a young nobleman, kinsman to the prince

MONTAGUE] heads of two houses at variance with each
CAPULET } other

An old man, of the Capulet family

ROMEO, son to Montague

MERCUTIO, kinsman to the prince, and friend to Romeo

BENVOLIO, nephew to Montague, and friend to Romeo

TYBALT, nephew to Lady Capulet

FRIAR LAURENCE, a Franciscan

FRIAR JOHN, of the same order

BALTHASAR, servant to Romeo

SAMPSON }
GREGORY } servants to Capulet

PETER, servant to Juliet's nurse

ABRAHAM, servant to Montague

An Apothecary

Three Musicians

Page to Paris; another Page; an Officer

LADY MONTAGUE, wife to Montague

LADY CAPULET, wife to Capulet

JULIET, daughter to Capulet

Nurse to Juliet

Citizens of Verona; kinsfolk of both houses; Maskers, Guards, Watchmen, and Attendants

SCENE: Verona; Mantua

THE PROLOGUE

Chorus.

Two households both alike in dignity,
(In fair Verona where we lay our scene)
From ancient grudge, break to new mutiny,   5
Where civil blood makes civil hands unclean:
From forth the fatal loins of these two foes,
A pair of star-cross'd lovers, take their life:
Whose misadventur'd piteous overthrows,
Doth with their death bury their parents' strife.   10
The fearful passage of their death-mark'd love,
And the continuance of their parents' rage:
Which but their children's end nought could remove:
Is now the two hours' traffic of our Stage.
The which if you with patient ears attend,   15
What here shall miss, our toil shall strive to mend.

Enter Sampson and Gregory, with swords and bucklers,
of the house of Capulet.

SAMPSON: Gregory, on my word we'll not carry coals.

5 GREGORY: No, for then we should be colliers.

SAMPSON: I mean, and we be in choler, we'll draw.

GREGORY: Ay while you live, draw your neck out of collar.

SAMPSON: I strike quickly being moved.

10 GREGORY: But thou art not quickly moved to strike.

SAMPSON: A dog of the house of Montague moves me.

GREGORY: To move is to stir, and to be valiant is to stand: therefore if thou art moved, thou runn'st away.

SAMPSON: A dog of that house shall move me to stand: I 15 will take the wall of any man or maid of Montague's.

GREGORY: That shows thee a weak slave, for the weakest goes to the wall.

SAMPSON: 'Tis true, and therefore women being the weaker vessels are ever thrust to the wall: therefore I will 20 push Montague's men from the wall, and thrust his maids to the wall.

GREGORY: The quarrel is between our masters, and us their men.

SAMPSON: 'Tis all one, I will show myself a tyrant: when 25 I have fought with the men, I will be civil with the maids, I will cut off their heads.

GREGORY: The heads of the maids.

SAMPSON: Ay the heads of the maids, or their maiden heads, take it in what sense you wilt.

30 GREGORY: They must take it sense that feel it.

SAMPSON: Me they shall feel while I am able to stand, and 'tis known I am a pretty piece of flesh.

GREGORY: 'Tis well thou art not fish, if thou hadst, thou hadst been poor John: draw thy tool, here comes of the house of Montagues.   5

Enter two other Serving men.

SAMPSON: My naked weapon is out, quarrel, I will back thee.

GREGORY: How, turn thy back and run?

SAMPSON: Fear me not.   10

GREGORY: No marry, I fear thee.

SAMPSON: Let us take the law of our sides, let them begin.

GREGORY: I will frown as I pass by, and let them take it as they list.

SAMPSON: Nay as they dare, I will bite my thumb at them,   15
which is disgrace to them if they bear it.

ABRAHAM: Do you bite your thumb at us sir?

SAMPSON: I do bite my thumb sir.

ABRAHAM: Do you bite your thumb at us sir?

SAMPSON: Is the law of our side if I say ay?   20

GREGORY: No.

SAMPSON: No sir, I do not bite my thumb at you sir, but I bite my thumb sir.

GREGORY: Do you quarrel sir?

ABRAHAM: Quarrel sir, no sir.   25

SAMPSON: But if you do sir, I am for you, I serve as good a man as you.

ABRAHAM: No better.

SAMPSON: Well sir.

Enter Benvolio.   30

GREGORY: Say better: here comes one of my master's kinsmen.

SAMPSON: Yes better sir.

ABRAHAM: You lie.

SAMPSON: Draw if you be men, Gregory, remember thy
5   washing blow.   *They fight.*

BENVOLIO: Part fools,
    Put up your swords, you know not what you do.
                  Enter Tybalt.

TYBALT: What art thou drawn among these heartless
10   hinds?
    Turn thee Benvolio, look upon thy death.

BENVOLIO: I do but keep the peace, put up thy sword,
    Or manage it to part these men with me.

TYBALT: What drawn and talk of peace? I hate the word,
15   As I hate hell, all Montagues and thee:
    Have at thee coward.
                They fight.
    Enter three or four Citizens with clubs or partisans.

OFFICER: Clubs, bills and partisans, strike, beat them down,
20   Down with the Capulets, down with the Montagues.
      Enter old Capulet in his gown, and his wife.

CAPULET: What noise is this? Give me my long sword ho.

LADY CAPULET: A crutch, a crutch, why call you for a
    sword?

25 CAPULET: My sword I say, old Montague is come,
    And flourishes his blade in spite of me.
        Enter old Montague and his wife.

MONTAGUE: Thou villain Capulet, hold me not, let me
    go.

30 LADY MONTAGUE: Thou shalt not stir one foot to seek a
    foe.   *Enter Prince Escales, with his train.*

PRINCE: Rebellious subjects enemies to peace,

Profaners of this neighbour-stained steel,
Will they not hear? What ho, you men, you beasts:
That quench the fire of your pernicious rage,
With purple fountains issuing from your veins:
On pain of torture from those bloody hands,   5
Throw your mistemper'd weapons to the ground,
And hear the sentence of your moved Prince.
Three civil brawls bred of an airy word,
By thee old Capulet and Montague,
Have thrice disturb'd the quiet of our streets,   10
And made Verona's ancient citizens,
Cast by their grave beseeming ornaments,
To wield old partisans, in hands as old,
Canker'd with peace, to part your canker'd hate.
If ever you disturb our streets again,   15
Your lives shall pay the forfeit of the peace.
For this time all the rest depart away:
You Capulet shall go along with me,
And Montague come you this afternoon,
To know our farther pleasure in this case: 20
To old Free-town, our common judgement place:
Once more on pain of death, all men depart.
Exeunt all but Montague, Lady Montague, and Benvolio.
MONTAGUE: Who set this ancient quarrel new abroach?
  Speak nephew, were you by when it began?   25
BENVOLIO: Here were the servants of your adversary
  And yours, close fighting ere I did approach,
  I drew to part them, in the instant came
  The fiery Tybalt, with his sword prepar'd,
  Which as he breath'd defiance to my ears,   30
  He swung about his head and cut the winds,
  Who nothing hurt withal, hiss'd him in scorn:

While we were interchanging thrusts and blows,
Came more and more, and fought on part and part,
Till the Prince came, who parted either part.

LADY MONTAGUE: O where is Romeo, saw you him to-
5   day?
Right glad I am, he was not at this fray.

BENVOLIO: Madam, an hour before the worshipp'd Sun,
Peer'd forth the golden window of the East,
A troubled mind drave me to walk abroad,
10   Where underneath the grove of sycamore,
That westward rooteth from this City side:
So early walking did I see your son,
Towards him I made, but he was ware of me,
And stole into the covert of the wood,
15   I measuring his affections by my own,
Which then most sought, where most might not be
     found,
Being one too many by my weary self,
Pursued my humour, not pursuing his,
20   And gladly shunn'd, who gladly fled from me.

MONTAGUE: Many a morning hath he there been seen,
With tears augmenting the fresh morning's dew,
Adding to clouds, more clouds with his deep sighs,
But all so soon as the all-cheering Sun,
25   Should in the farthest East begin to draw
The shady curtains from Aurora's bed,
Away from light steals home my heavy son,
And private in his chamber pens himself,
Shuts up his windows, locks fair daylight out,
30   And makes himself an artificial night:
Black and portentous must this humour prove,
Unless good counsel may the cause remove.

BENVOLIO: My noble uncle do you know the cause?

MONTAGUE: I neither know it, nor can learn of him.

BENVOLIO: Have you importun'd him by any means?

MONTAGUE: Both by myself and many other friends,
  But he his own affections' counsellor,   5
  Is to himself (I will not say how true)
  But to himself so secret and so close,
  So far from sounding and discovery,
  As is the bud bit with an envious worm,
  Ere he can spread his sweet leaves to the air,   10
  Or dedicate his beauty to the same.
  Could we but learn from whence his sorrows grow,
  We would as willingly give cure as know.

Enter Romeo.

BENVOLIO: See where he comes, so please you step aside, 15
  I'll know his grievance or be much denied.

MONTAGUE: I would thou wert so happy by thy stay,
  To hear true shrift, come Madam let's away.

Exeunt.

BENVOLIO: Good morrow Cousin.   20

ROMEO: Is the day so young?

BENVOLIO: But new struck nine.

ROMEO: Ay me, sad hours seem long:
  Was that my father that went hence so fast?

BENVOLIO: It was: what sadness lengthens Romeo's hours? 25

ROMEO: Not having that, which having, makes them short.

BENVOLIO: In love.

ROMEO: Out.

BENVOLIO: Of love.

ROMEO: Out of her favour where I am in love.   30

BENVOLIO: **Alas that love so gentle in his view,**
  Should be so tyrannous and rough in proof.

ROMEO: Alas that love, whose view is muffled still,
Should without eyes, see pathways to his will:
Where shall we dine? O me! what fray was here?
Yet tell me not, for I have heard it all:
5 Here's much to do with hate, but more with love:
Why then O brawling love, O loving hate,
O any thing of nothing first created:
O heavy lightness, serious vanity,
Mis-shapen Chaos of well-seeming forms,
10 Feather of lead, bright smoke, cold fire, sick health,
Still-waking sleep that is not what it is.
This love feel I, that feel no love in this,
Dost thou not laugh?

BENVOLIO: No coz, I rather weep.

15 ROMEO: Good heart at what?

BENVOLIO: At thy good heart's oppression.

ROMEO: Why such is love's transgression:
Griefs of mine own lie heavy in my breast,
Which thou wilt propagate to have it press'd,
20 With more of thine, this love that thou hast shown,
Doth add more grief, to too much of mine own.
Love is a smoke made with the fume of sighs,
Being purg'd, a fire sparkling in lovers' eyes,
Being vex'd, a sea nourish'd with loving tears,
25 What is it else? A madness, most discreet,
A choking gall, and a preserving sweet:
Farewell my coz.

BENVOLIO: Soft I will go along:
And if you leave me so, you do me wrong.

30 ROMEO: Tut I have lost myself, I am not here,
This is not Romeo, he's some other where.

BENVOLIO: Tell me in sadness, who is that you love?

ROMEO: What shall I groan and tell thee?

BENVOLIO: Groan, why no: but sadly tell me who.

ROMEO: Bid a sick man in sadness make his will:
  A word ill urg'd to one that is so ill:
  In sadness cousin, I do love a woman.   5

BENVOLIO: I aim'd so near, when I suppos'd you lov'd.

ROMEO: A right good mark-man, and she's fair I love.

BENVOLIO: A right fair mark fair coz is soonest hit.

ROMEO: Well in that hit you miss, she'll not be hit
  With Cupid's arrow, she hath Dian's wit: 10
  And in strong proof of chastity well arm'd,
  From love's weak childish bow she lives uncharm'd
  She will not stay the siege of loving terms,
  Nor bide th' incounter of assailing eyes.
  Nor ope her lap to saint-seducing gold,   15
  O she is rich in beauty, only poor,
  That when she dies, with beauty dies her store.

BENVOLIO: Then she hath sworn, that she will still live
chaste?

ROMEO: She hath, and in that sparing, makes huge waste: 20
  For beauty starv'd with her severity,
  Cuts beauty off from all posterity.
  She is too fair, too wise, wisely too fair,
  To merit bliss by making me despair:
  She hath forsworn to love, and in that vow,   25
  Do I live dead, that live to tell it now.

BENVOLIO: Be rul'd by me, forget to think of her.

ROMEO: O teach me how I should forget to think.

BENVOLIO: By giving liberty unto thine eyes,
  Examine other beauties.   30

ROMEO: 'Tis the way
  To call hers, exquisite, in question more:

These happy masks that kiss fair Ladies' brows,
Being black, puts us in mind they hide the fair:
He that is strucken blind, cannot forget
The precious treasure of his eyesight lost;
5 Show me a mistress that is passing fair,
What doth her beauty serve but as a note,
Where I may read who pass'd that passing fair:
Farewell, thou canst not teach me to forget.
BENVOLIO: I'll pay that doctrine, or else die in debt.
10   *Exeunt.*

I. 2

Enter Capulet, County Paris, and the Clown.
CAPULET: But Montague is bound as well as I,
In penalty alike, and 'tis not hard I think,
15 For men so old as we to keep the peace.
PARIS: Of honourable reckoning are you both,
And pity 'tis, you liv'd at odds so long:
But now my Lord, what say you to my suit?
CAPULET: But saying o'er what I have said before,
20 My child is yet a stranger in the world,
She hath not seen the change of fourteen years,
Let two more summers wither in their pride,
Ere we may think her ripe to be a bride.
PARIS: Younger than she, are happy mothers made.
25 CAPULET: And too soon marr'd are those so early made:
The earth hath swallowed all my hopes but she,
She is the hopeful Lady of my earth:
But woo her gentle Paris, get her heart,
My will to her consent, is but a part.

And she agreed, within her scope of choice
Lies my consent, and fair according voice:
This night I hold an old accustom'd feast,
Whereto I have invited many a guest:
Such as I love, and you among the store,   5
One more, most welcome makes my number more:
At my poor house, look to behold this night,
Earth-treading stars, that make dark heaven light:
Such comfort as do lusty young men feel,
When well-apparell'd April on the heel,   10
Of limping winter treads, even such delight
Among fresh female buds shall you this night
Inherit at my house, hear all, all see:
And like her most, whose merit most shall be:
Which on more view, of many, mine being one,   15
May stand in number, though in reckoning none.
Come go with me, go sirrah trudge about,
Through fair Verona, find those persons out,
Whose names are written there, and to them say,
My house and welcome, on their pleasure stay.   20

                    Exeunt Capulet and Paris.

CLOWN: Find them out whose names are written. Here it
  is written, that the shoemaker should meddle with his
  yard, and the tailor with his last, the fisher with his pencil,
  and the painter with his nets. But I am sent to find those   25
  persons whose names are here writ, and can never find
  what names the writing person hath here writ. I must to
  the learned: in good time.

                  Enter Benvolio and Romeo.

BENVOLIO: Tut man, one fire burns out another's burn-   30
  ing,
  One pain is lessen'd by another's anguish,

Turn giddy, and be holp by backward turning:
One desperate grief, cures with another's languish:
Take thou some new infection to thy eye,
And the rank poison of the old will die.

5 ROMEO: Your plantain-leaf is excellent for that.

BENVOLIO: For what I pray thee?

ROMEO: For your broken shin.

BENVOLIO: Why Romeo, art thou mad?

ROMEO: Not mad, but bound more than a madman is:

10 Shut up in prison, kept without my food,
Whipt and tormented, and God-den good fellow.

CLOWN: God gi' god-den, I pray sir can you read?

ROMEO: Ay mine own fortune in my misery.

CLOWN: Perhaps you have learned it without book: but I

15 pray can you read anything you see?

ROMEO: Ay if I know the letters and the language.

CLOWN: Ye say honestly, rest you merry.

ROMEO: Stay fellow, I can read.

He reads the letter.

20 *Seigneur Martino, and his wife and daughters: County An-*
selme and his beauteous sisters: the Lady widow of Vitruvio,
Seigneur Placentio, and his lovely nieces: Mercutio and his
brother Valentine: mine Uncle Capulet, his wife and daught-
ers: my fair Niece Rosaline, Livia, Seigneur Valentio and his

25 *cousin Tybalt: Lucio and the lively Helena.*

A fair assembly, whither should they come?

CLOWN: Up.

ROMEO: Whither to supper?

CLOWN: To our house.

30 ROMEO: Whose house?

CLOWN: My master's.

ROMEO: Indeed I should have ask'd you that before.

CLOWN: Now I'll tell you without asking. My master is
the great rich Capulet, and if you be not of the house of
Montagues, I pray come and crush a cup of wine. Rest
you merry.

                                   Exit.   5

BENVOLIO: At this same ancient feast of Capulet's,
Sups the fair Rosaline whom thou so loves:
With all the admired beauties of Verona,
Go thither, and with unattainted eye,
Compare her face with some that I shall show,   10
And I will make thee think thy swan a crow.

ROMEO: When the devout religion of mine eye,
Maintains such falsehood, then turn tears to fires:
And these who often drown'd, could never die,
Transparent heretics be burnt for liars.   15
One fairer than my love, the all-seeing Sun,
Ne'er saw her match, since first the world begun.

BENVOLIO: Tut you saw her fair none else being by,
Herself pois'd with herself in either eye:
But in that crystal scales let there be weigh'd,   20
Your lady's love against some other maid:
That I will show you shining at this feast,
And she shall scant show well that now seems best.

ROMEO: I'll go along no such sight to be shown,
But to rejoice in splendour of mine own.   25

                                  Exeunt.

I. 3

Enter Lady Capulet and Nurse.

LADY CAPULET: Nurse where's my daughter? Call her
forth to me.   30

NURSE: Now by my maidenhead at twelve year old, I
bade her come, what lamb, what lady-bird, God forbid,
where's this girl? What Juliet.

Enter Juliet.

5 JULIET: How now who calls?

NURSE: Your mother.

JULIET: Madam I am here, what is your will?

LADY CAPULET: This is the matter. Nurse give leave a-
while, we must talk in secret. Nurse come back again, I

10 have remember'd me, thou's hear our counsel. Thou
knowest my daughter's of a pretty age.

NURSE: Faith I can tell her age unto an hour.

LADY CAPULET: She's not fourteen.

NURSE: I'll lay fourteen of my teeth, and yet to my teen

15 be it spoken, I have but four, she is not fourteen. How
long is it now to Lammas-tide?

LADY CAPULET: A fortnight and odd days.

NURSE: Even or odd, of all days in the year come Lammas-
Eve at night, shall she be fourteen. Susan and she, God

20 rest all Christian souls, were of an age. Well Susan is with
God, she was too good for me: but as I said, on Lammas-
Eve at night shall she be fourteen, that shall she marry,
I remember it well. 'Tis since the Earthquake now eleven
years, and she was wean'd I never shall forget it, of all the

25 days of the year upon that day: for I had then laid wormwood to my dug, sitting in the sun under the dove-house
wall. My Lord and you were then at Mantua, nay I do
bear a brain. But as I said, when it did taste the wormwood on the nipple of my dug, and felt it bitter, pretty

30 fool, to see it tetchy, and fall out with the dug. Shake
quoth the dove-house, 'twas no need I trow to bid me
trudge: and since that time it is eleven years, for then she

could stand high-lone, nay by th' rood she could have
run and waddled all about: for even the day before she
broke her brow, and then my husband, God be with his
soul, a' was a merry man, took up the child, Yea quoth
he, dost thou fall upon thy face? Thou wilt fall backward   5
when thou hast more wit, wilt thou not Jule? And by my
holidame, the pretty wretch left crying, and said ay: to
see now how a jest shall come about: I warrant, and I
should live a thousand years, I never should forget it: wilt
thou not Jule quoth he? And pretty fool it stinted, and   10
said ay.

LADY CAPULET: Enough of this, I pray thee hold thy
peace.

NURSE: Yes Madam, yet I cannot choose but laugh, to
think it should leave crying, and say ay: and yet I warrant   15
it had upon it brow, a bump as big as a young cockerel's
stone: a perilous knock, and it cried bitterly. Yea quoth
my husband, fall'st upon thy face, thou wilt fall backward when thou comest to age: wilt thou not Jule? It
stinted, and said ay.   20

JULIET: And stint thou too, I pray thee Nurse, say I.

NURSE: Peace I have done: God mark thee to his grace,
thou wast the prettiest babe that e'er I nurs'd, and I might
live to see thee married once, I have my wish.

LADY CAPULET: Marry, that marry is the very theme   25
I came to talk of, tell me daughter Juliet,
How stands your disposition to be married?

JULIET: It is an honour that I dream not of.

NURSE: An honour, were not I thine only Nurse, I would
say thou hadst suck'd wisdom from thy teat.   30

LADY CAPULET: Well think of marriage now, younger
than you

Here in Verona, Ladies of esteem,
Are made already mothers by my count.
I was your mother, much upon these years
That you are now a maid: thus then in brief,
5   The valiant Paris seeks you for his love.

NURSE: A man young Lady, Lady, such a man as all the
world. Why he's a man of wax.

LADY CAPULET: Verona's summer hath not such a flower.

NURSE: Nay he's a flower in faith a very flower.

10   LADY CAPULET: What say you, can you love the gentleman?

This night you shall behold him at our feast,
Read o'er the volume of young Paris' face,
And find delight, writ there with beauty's pen,
15   Examine every married lineament,
And see how one another lends content:
And what obscur'd in this fair volume lies,
Find written in the margent of his eyes.
This precious book of love, this unbound lover,
20   To beautify him, only lacks a cover:
The fish lives in the sea, and 'tis much pride
For fair without the fair, within to hide:
That book in many's eyes doth share the glory
That in gold clasps locks in the golden story:
25   So shall you share all that he doth possess,
By having him, making yourself no less.

NURSE: No less, nay bigger women grow by men.

LADY CAPULET: Speak briefly, can you like of Paris' love?

JULIET: I'll look to like, if looking liking move.
30   But no more deep will I endart mine eye,
Than your consent gives strength to make it fly.
                              Enter Servingman.

SERVINGMAN: Madam the guests are come, supper serv'd
up, you call'd, my young Lady ask'd for, the Nurse curs'd
in the Pantry, and every thing in extremity: I must hence
to wait, I beseech you follow straight.

LADY CAPULET: We follow thee, Juliet the County stays. 5

NURSE: Go girl, seek happy nights to happy days.
Exeunt.

I. 4

*Enter Romeo, Mercutio, Benvolio, with five or six other
Maskers, Torch-bearers.* 10

ROMEO: What shall this speech be spoke for our excuse?
Or shall we on without apology?

BENVOLIO: The date is out of such prolixity,
We'll have no Cupid, hoodwink'd with a scarf,
Bearing a Tartar's painted bow of lath, 15
Scaring the Ladies like a crow-keeper.
Nor no without-book prologue faintly spoke
After the prompter, for our entrance.
But let them measure us by what they will,
We'll measure them a measure and be gone. 20

ROMEO: Give me a torch, I am not for this ambling,
Being but heavy I will bear the light.

MERCUTIO: Nay gentle Romeo, we must have you dance.

ROMEO: Not I believe me, you have dancing shoes
With nimble soles, I have a soul of lead 25
So stakes me to the ground I cannot move.

MERCUTIO: You are a lover, borrow Cupid's wings,
And soar with them above a common bound.

ROMEO: I am too sore enpierced with his shaft,

To soar with his light feathers and so bound,
I cannot bound a pitch above dull woe,
Under love's heavy burthen do I sink.

MERCUTIO: And to sink in it should you burthen love,
5   Too great oppression for a tender thing.

ROMEO: Is love a tender thing? It is too rough,
Too rude, too boisterous, and it pricks like thorn.

MERCUTIO: If love be rough with you, be rough with
        love,
10   Prick love for pricking, and you beat love down,
Give me a case to put my visage in,
A visor for a visor, what care I
What curious eye doth cote deformities:
Here are the beetle-brows shall blush for me.

15 BENVOLIO: Come knock and enter, and no sooner in,
But every man betake him to his legs.

ROMEO: A torch for me, let wantons light of heart
Tickle the senseless rushes with their heels:
For I am proverb'd with a grandsire phrase,
20   I'll be a candle-holder and look on,
The game was ne'er so fair, and I am done.

MERCUTIO: Tut, dun's the mouse, the constable's own
        word:
If thou art dun, we'll draw thee from the mire,
25   Or save your reverence love, wherein thou stick'st
Up to the ears, come we burn daylight ho.

ROMEO: Nay that's not so.

MERCUTIO: I mean sir in delay
We waste our lights in vain, lights, lights, by day:
30   Take our good meaning, for our judgement sits,
Five times in that, ere once in our fine wits.

ROMEO: And we mean well in going to this Mask,

But 'tis no wit to go.
MERCUTIO: Why, may one ask?
ROMEO: I dreamt a dream to-night.
MERCUTIO: And so did I.
ROMEO: Well what was yours?   5
MERCUTIO: That dreamers often lie.
ROMEO: In bed asleep while they do dream things true.
MERCUTIO: O then I see Queen Mab hath been with you:
  She is the Fairies' midwife, and she comes
  In shape no bigger than an agate-stone,   10
  On the forefinger of an alderman,
  Drawn with a team of little atomies,
  Over men's noses as they lie asleep:
  Her waggon-spokes made of long spinners' legs:
  The cover, of the wings of grasshoppers,   15
  Her traces of the smallest spiders web,
  Her collars of the moonshine's watery beams,
  Her whip of cricket's bone, the lash of film,
  Her waggoner, a small grey-coated gnat,
  Not half so big as a round little worm,   20
  Prick'd from the lazy finger of a maid.
  Her chariot is an empty hazel-nut,
  Made by the joiner squirrel or old grub,
  Time out o' mind, the Fairies' coachmakers:
  And in this state she gallops night by night,   25
  Through lovers' brains, and then they dream of love,
  On courtiers' knees, that dream on court'sies straight,
  O'er lawyers' fingers who straight dream on fees,
  O'er ladies' lips who straight on kisses dream,
  Which oft the angry Mab with blisters plagues,   30
  Because their breaths with sweetmeats tainted are.
  Sometime she gallops o'er a courtier's nose,

And then dreams he of smelling out a suit:
And sometime comes she with a tithe-pig's tail,
Tickling a parson's nose as a' lies asleep,
Then he dreams of another benefice.
5   Sometime she driveth o'er a soldier's neck,
And then dreams he of cutting foreign throats,
Of breaches, ambuscadoes, Spanish blades:
Of healths five fadom deep, and then anon
Drums in his ear, at which he starts and wakes,
10 And being thus frighted, swears a prayer or two
And sleeps again: this is that very Mab
That plats the manes of horses in the night:
And bakes the elf-locks in foul sluttish hairs,
Which once untangled, much misfortune bodes.
15 This is the hag, when maids lie on their backs,
That presses them and learns them first to bear,
Making them women of good carriage:
This is she.
ROMEO: Peace, peace, Mercutio peace,
20 Thou talk'st of nothing.
MERCUTIO: True, I talk of dreams:
Which are the children of an idle brain,
Begot of nothing but vain fantasy:
Which is as thin of substance as the air,
25 And more inconstant than the wind who woos
Even now the frozen bosom of the North:
And being anger'd puffs away from thence,
Turning his side to the dew-dropping South.
BENVOLIO: This wind you talk of, blows us from our-
30 selves,
Supper is done, and we shall come too late.
ROMEO: I fear too early, for my mind misgives,

Some consequence yet hanging in the stars,
Shall bitterly begin his fearful date,
With this night's revels, and expire the term
Of a despised life clos'd in my breast,
By some vile forfeit of untimely death.   5
But He that hath the steerage of my course,
Direct my sail: on lusty gentlemen.
BENVOLIO: Strike drum.

They march about the stage, and servingmen come forth
with napkins.   10

I.5

Enter Servant.

SERVANT: Where's Potpan that he helps not to take away?
He shift a trencher, he scrape a trencher?
1 SERVINGMAN: When good manners shall lie all in one   15
or two men's hands, and they unwash'd too, 'tis a foul
thing.
SERVANT: Away with the joint-stools, remove the court-
cupboard, look to the plate: good thou, save me a piece
of marchpane, and as thou loves me, let the porter let in 20
Susan Grindstone, and Nell, Antony and Potpan.
2 SERVINGMAN: Ay boy ready.
SERVANT: You are look'd for, and call'd for, ask'd for, and
sought for in the great chamber.
3 SERVINGMAN: We cannot be here and there too, cheer- 25
ly boys, be brisk a while, and the longer liver take all.
Exeunt.

Enter old Capulet with all the guests and gentlewomen
to the Maskers.

CAPULET: Welcome gentlemen, Ladies that have their toes 30

Unplagued with corns, will walk about with you:
Ah my mistresses, which of you all
Will now deny to dance? She that makes dainty,
She I'll swear hath corns: am I come near ye now?
5 Welcome gentlemen, I have seen the day
That I have worn a visor, and could tell
A whispering tale in a fair Lady's ear:
Such as would please: 'tis gone, 'tis gone, 'tis gone,
You are welcome, gentlemen come, musicians play.
10   *Music plays and they dance.*
A hall, a hall, give room, and foot it girls,
More light you knaves, and turn the tables up:
And quench the fire, the room is grown too hot.
Ah sirrah, this unlook'd-for sport comes well:
15 Nay sit, nay sit, good cousin Capulet,
For you and I are past our dancing days:
How long is 't now since last yourself and I
Were in a mask?
      2 CAPULET: Berlady thirty years.
20 CAPULET: What man 'tis not so much, 'tis not so much,
'Tis since the nuptial of Lucentio:
Come Pentecost as quickly as it will,
Some five and twenty years, and then we mask'd.
      2 CAPULET: 'Tis more, 'tis more, his son is elder sir:
25 His son is thirty.
      CAPULET: Will you tell me that?
His son was but a ward two years ago.
      ROMEO: What Lady's that which doth enrich the hand
Of yonder knight?
30 SERVANT: I know not sir.
      ROMEO: O she doth teach the torches to burn bright:
It seems she hangs upon the cheek of night,

As a rich jewel in an Ethiop's ear:
Beauty too rich for use, for earth too dear:
So shows a snowy dove trooping with crows,
As yonder Lady o'er her fellows shows.
The measure done, I'll watch her place of stand,   5
And touching hers, make blessed my rude hand.
Did my heart love till now, forswear it sight,
For I ne'er saw true beauty till this night.

TYBALT: This by his voice, should be a Montague.
Fetch me my rapier boy, what dares the slave   10
Come hither, cover'd with an antic face,
To fleer and scorn at our solemnity?
Now by the stock and honour of my kin,
To strike him dead, I hold it not a sin.

CAPULET: Why how now kinsman, wherefore storm you   15
so?

TYBALT: Uncle, this is a Montague our foe:
A villain that is hither come in spite,
To scorn at our solemnity this night.

CAPULET: Young Romeo is it?   20

TYBALT: 'Tis he, that villain Romeo.

CAPULET: Content thee gentle coz, let him alone,
A' bears him like a portly gentleman:
And to say truth, Verona brags of him,
To be a virtuous and well-govern'd youth: 25
I would not for the wealth of all this town,
Here in my house do him disparagement.
Therefore be patient, take no note of him,
It is my will, the which if you respect,
Show a fair presence, and put off these frowns,   30
An ill-beseeming semblance for a feast.

TYBALT: It fits when such a villain is a guest.

I'll not endure him.

CAPULET: He shall be endured.

What goodman boy, I say he shall, go to,

Am I the master here or you? go to,

5   You'll not endure him, God shall mend my soul,

You'll make a mutiny among my guests:

You will set cock-a-hoop, you'll be the man.

TYBALT: Why uncle, 'tis a shame.

CAPULET: Go to, go to,

10   You are a saucy boy, is't so indeed?

This trick may chance to scathe you I know what,

You must contrary me, marry 'tis time,

Well said my hearts, you are a princox, go,

Be quiet, or more light, more light for shame,

15   I'll make you quiet. What, cheerly my hearts.

TYBALT: Patience perforce, with wilful choler meeting,

Makes my flesh tremble in their different greeting:

I will withdraw, but this intrusion shall

Now seeming sweet, convert to bitt'rest gall.

20   *Exit.*

ROMEO: If I profane with my unworthiest hand,

This holy shrine, the gentle sin is this,

My lips two blushing Pilgrims ready stand,

To smooth the rough touch with a gentle kiss.

25   JULIET: Good Pilgrim you do wrong your hand too much

Which mannerly devotion shows in this,

For saints have hands, that Pilgrims' hands do touch,

And palm to palm is holy Palmers' kiss.

ROMEO: Have not Saints lips and holy Palmers too?

30   JULIET: Ay Pilgrim, lips that they must use in prayer.

ROMEO: O then dear Saint, let lips do what hands do,

They pray, grant thou, lest faith turn to despair.

JULIET: Saints do not move, though grant for prayers' sake.

ROMEO: Then move not while my prayer's effect I take,
Thus from my lips, by thine my sin is purg'd.

JULIET: Then have my lips the sin that they have took.

ROMEO: Sin from my lips, O trespass sweetly urg'd: 5
Give me my sin again.

JULIET: You kiss by th' book.

NURSE: Madam your mother craves a word with you.

ROMEO: What is her mother?

NURSE: Marry bachelor,   10
Her mother is the Lady of the house,
And a good Lady, and a wise and virtuous,
I nurs'd her daughter that you talk'd withal:
I tell you, he that can lay hold of her
Shall have the chinks.   15

ROMEO: Is she a Capulet?
O dear account! my life is my foe's debt.

BENVOLIO: Away be gone, the sport is at the best.

ROMEO: Ay so I fear, the more is my unrest.

CAPULET: Nay gentlemen prepare not to be gone,   20
We have a trifling foolish banquet towards:
Is it e'en so? Why then I thank you all.
I thank you honest gentlemen, good night:
More torches here, come on, then let's to bed.
Ah sirrah, by my fay it waxes late,   25
I'll to my rest.

JULIET: Come hither Nurse, what is yond gentleman?

NURSE: The son and heir of old Tiberio.

JULIET: What's he that now is going out of door?

NURSE: Marry that I think be young Petruchio.   30

JULIET: What's he that follows there that would not
dance?

NURSE: I know not.

JULIET: Go ask his name, if he be married,
My grave is like to be my wedding bed.

NURSE: His name is Romeo, and a Montague,
5   The only son of your great enemy.

JULIET: My only love sprung from my only hate,
Too early seen, unknown, and known too late,
Prodigious birth of love it is to me,
That I must love a loathed enemy.

10 NURSE: What's this? What's this?

JULIET: A rhyme I learn'd even now
Of one I danc'd withal.

One calls within: Juliet.

NURSE: Anon, anon:
15   Come let's away, the strangers all are gone.

Exeunt.

II

Chorus.

Now old desire doth in his death-bed lie,
20   And young affection gapes to be his heir,
That fair for which love groan'd for and would die,
With tender Juliet match'd, is now not fair.
Now Romeo is beloved, and loves again,
Alike bewitched by the charm of looks:
25   But to his foe suppos'd he must complain,
And she steal love's sweet bait from fearful hooks:
Being held a foe, he may not have access
To breathe such vows as lovers use to swear,
And she as much in love, her means much less,

To meet her new beloved any where:
But passion lends them power, time means to meet,
Tempering extremities with extreme sweet.

Exit.

II. 1   5

Enter Romeo alone.

ROMEO: Can I go forward when my heart is here,
Turn back dull earth and find thy centre out.

[*He hides.*]

Enter Benvolio with Mercutio.   10

BENVOLIO: Romeo, my cousin Romeo, Romeo.

MERCUTIO: He is wise, and on my life hath stol'n him
home to bed.

BENVOLIO: He ran this way and leap'd this orchard wall.
Call good Mercutio.   15

MERCUTIO: Nay I'll conjure too.
Romeo, humours, madman, passion, lover,
Appear thou in the likeness of a sigh,
Speak but one rhyme and I am satisfied:
Cry but ay me, pronounce but love and dove,   20
Speak to my gossip Venus one fair word,
One nickname for her purblind son and her
Young Abraham Cupid he that shot so true
When King Cophetua lov'd the beggar-maid.
He heareth not, he stirreth not, he moveth not   25
The ape is dead, and I must conjure him.
I conjure thee by Rosaline's bright eyes,
By her high forehead, and her scarlet lip,
By her fine foot, straight leg, and quivering thigh,
And the demesnes, that there adjacent lie,   30

That in thy likeness thou appear to us.

BENVOLIO: And if he hear thee thou wilt anger him.

MERCUTIO: This cannot anger him, 'twould anger him
　　To raise a spirit in his mistress' circle,
5　　Of some strange nature, letting it there stand
　　Till she had laid it, and conjur'd it down,
　　That were some spite. My invocation
　　Is fair and honest, in his mistress' name,
　　I conjure only but to raise up him.

10 BENVOLIO: Come, he hath hid himself among these trees
　　To be consorted with the humorous night:
　　Blind is his love, and best befits the dark.

MERCUTIO: If love be blind love cannot hit the mark:
　　Now will he sit under a medlar-tree,
15　　And wish his mistress were that kind of fruit,
　　As maids call medlars, when they laugh alone.
　　O Romeo that she were, O that she were
　　An open et cetera, or thou a poperin pear.
　　Romeo good night, I'll to my truckle-bed,
20　　This field-bed is too cold for me to sleep,
　　Come shall we go?

BENVOLIO: Go then, for 'tis in vain
　　To seek him here that means not to be found.

Exeunt.

25　　# II.2

[Romeo comes forth.]

ROMEO: He jests at scars that never felt a wound.

[Juliet appears at the window.]

　　But soft, what light through yonder window breaks?
30　　It is the East, and Juliet is the Sun.

Arise fair Sun and kill the envious Moon,
Who is already sick and pale with grief,
That thou her maid art far more fair than she:
Be not her maid since she is envious,
Her vestal livery is but sick and green,   5
And none but fools do wear it, cast it off:
It is my Lady, O it is my love,
O that she knew she were,
She speaks, yet she says nothing, what of that?
Her eye discourses, I will answer it: 10
I am too bold, 'tis not to me she speaks:
Two of the fairest stars in all the heaven,
Having some business do intreat her eyes,
To twinkle in their spheres till they return.
What if her eyes were there, they in her head,   15
The brightness of her cheek would shame those stars,
As daylight doth a lamp, her eye in heaven
Would through the airy region stream so bright,
That birds would sing, and think it were not night:
See how she leans her cheek upon her hand.   20
O that I were a glove upon that hand,
That I might touch that cheek.
JULIET: Ay me.
ROMEO: She speaks.
  Oh speak again bright Angel, for thou art   25
As glorious to this night being o'er my head,
As is a winged messenger of heaven
Unto the white-upturned wondering eyes,
Of mortals that fall back to gaze on him,
When he bestrides the lazy puffing clouds,   30
And sails upon the bosom of the air.
JULIET: O Romeo, Romeo, wherefore art thou Romeo?

Deny thy father and refuse thy name.
Or if thou wilt not, be but sworn my love,
And I'll no longer be a Capulet.

ROMEO: Shall I hear more, or shall I speak at this?

5 JULIET: 'Tis but thy name that is my enemy:
Thou art thyself, though not a Montague,
What's Montague? It is nor hand nor foot,
Nor arm nor face, nor any other part
Belonging to a man. O be some other name.

10 What's in a name? That which we call a rose,
By any other name would smell as sweet,
So Romeo would were he not Romeo call'd,
Retain that dear perfection which he owes,
Without that title, Romeo doff thy name,

15 And for thy name which is no part of thee,
Take all my self.

ROMEO: I take thee at thy word:
Call me but love, and I'll be new baptiz'd,
Henceforth I never will be Romeo.

20 JULIET: What man art thou, that thus bescreen'd in night
So stumblest on my counsel?

ROMEO: By a name,
I know not how to tell thee who I am:
My name dear saint, is hateful to myself,

25 Because it is an enemy to thee;
Had I it written, I would tear the word.

JULIET: My ears have yet not drunk a hundred words
Of thy tongue's uttering, yet I know the sound.
Art thou not Romeo, and a Montague?

30 ROMEO: Neither fair maid, if either thee dislike.

JULIET: How cam'st thou hither, tell me, and wherefore?
The orchard walls are high and hard to climb,

And the place death, considering who thou art,
If any of my kinsmen find thee here.
ROMEO: With love's light wings did I o'er-perch these
    walls,
For stony limits cannot hold love out,   5
And what love can do, that dares love attempt:
Therefore thy kinsmen are no stop to me.
JULIET: If they do see thee, they will murther thee.
ROMEO: Alack there lies more peril in thine eye,
Than twenty of their swords, look thou but sweet,   10
And I am proof against their enmity.
JULIET: I would not for the world they saw thee here.
ROMEO: I have night's cloak to hide me from their eyes,
And but thou love me, let them find me here,
My life were better ended by their hate,   15
Than death prorogued wanting of thy love.
JULIET: By whose directions found'st thou out this place?
ROMEO: By love that first did prompt me to inquire,
He lent me counsel, and I lent him eyes:
I am no pilot, yet wert thou as far   20
As that vast shore wash'd with the farthest sea,
I should adventure for such merchandise.
JULIET: Thou know'st the mask of night is on my face,
Else would a maiden blush bepaint my cheek,
For that which thou hast heard me speak to-night,   25
Fain would I dwell on form, fain, fain, deny
What I have spoke, but farewell compliment.
Dost thou love me? I know thou wilt say ay:
And I will take thy word, yet if thou swear'st,
Thou mayst prove false: at lover's perjuries   30
They say Jove laughs; O gentle Romeo,
If thou dost love, pronounce it faithfully:

Or if thou thinkest I am too quickly won,
I'll frown and be perverse, and say thee nay,
So thou wilt woo, but else not for the world,
In truth fair Montague, I am too fond:
5 And therefore thou mayst think my 'haviour light,
But trust me gentleman, I'll prove more true,
Than those that have more cunning to be strange:
I should have been more strange, I must confess,
But that thou overheard'st ere I was ware,
10 My true love passion, therefore pardon me,
And not impute this yielding to light love,
Which the dark night hath so discovered.

ROMEO: Lady, by yonder blessed Moon I vow,
That tips with silver all these fruit-tree tops.

15 JULIET: O swear not by the Moon th' inconstant Moon,
That monthly changes in her circled orb,
Lest that thy love prove likewise variable.

ROMEO: What shall I swear by?

JULIET: Do not swear at all:
20 Or if thou wilt, swear by thy gracious self,
Which is the god of my idolatry,
And I'll believe thee.

ROMEO: If my heart's dear love –

JULIET: Well do not swear, although I joy in thee:
25 I have no joy of this contract to-night,
It is too rash, too unadvis'd, too sudden,
Too like the lightning which doth cease to be,
Ere one can say, it lightens. Sweet, good night:
This bud of love by summer's ripening breath,
30 May prove a beauteous flower when next we meet:
Good night, good night, as sweet repose and rest,
Come to thy heart, as that within my breast.

ROMEO: O wilt thou leave me so unsatisfied?

JULIET: What satisfaction canst thou have to-night?

ROMEO: Th' exchange of thy Love's faithful vow for mine.

JULIET: I gave thee mine before thou didst request it:
And yet I would it were to give again.   5

ROMEO: Wouldst thou withdraw it, for what purpose
Love?

JULIET: But to be frank and give it thee again,
And yet I wish but for the thing I have,
My bounty is as boundless as the sea,   10
My love as deep, the more I give to thee
The more I have, for both are infinite.
I hear some noise within, dear love adieu:
                    Calls within.
Anon good Nurse, sweet Montague, be true: 15
Stay but a little, I will come again.

ROMEO: O blessed blessed night, I am afeard
Being in night, all this is but a dream,
Too flattering-sweet to be substantial.

JULIET: Three words dear Romeo, and good night in-   20
deed:
If that thy bent of love be honourable,
Thy purpose marriage, send me word to-morrow,
By one that I'll procure to come to thee,
Where and what time thou wilt perform the rite,   25
And all my fortunes at thy foot I'll lay,
And follow thee my Lord throughout the world.
                    Within: Madam.

JULIET: I come, anon: but if thou mean'st not well,
I do beseech thee.   30
                    Within: Madam.

JULIET: (By and by I come)

To cease thy strife, and leave me to my grief,
To-morrow will I send.

ROMEO: So thrive my soul.

JULIET: A thousand times good night.

5   *Exit.*

ROMEO: A thousand times the worse to want thy light,
Love goes toward love as schoolboys from their books,
But love from love, toward school with heavy looks.

Enter Juliet again.

10 JULIET: Hist Romeo hist: O for a falconer's voice,
To lure this tassel-gentle back again,
Bondage is hoarse, and may not speak aloud,
Else would I tear the cave where Echo lies,
And make her airy tongue more hoarse than mine,
15 With repetition of my Romeo's name.

ROMEO: It is my soul that calls upon my name.
How silver-sweet, sound lovers' tongues by night,
Like softest music to attending ears.

JULIET: Romeo.

20 ROMEO: My niece.

JULIET: At what o'clock to-morrow
Shall I send to thee?

ROMEO: By the hour of nine.

JULIET: I will not fail, 'tis twenty years till then,
25 I have forgot why I did call thee back.

ROMEO: Let me stand here till thou remember it.

JULIET: I shall forget to have thee still stand there,
Remembering how I love thy company.

ROMEO: And I'll still stay, to have thee still forget,
30 Forgetting any other home but this.

JULIET: 'Tis almost morning, I would have thee gone,
And yet no farther than a wanton's bird

That lets it hop a little from his hand,
Like a poor prisoner in his twisted gyves,
And with a silken thread, plucks it back again,
So loving-jealous of his liberty.

ROMEO: I would I were thy bird. 5

JULIET: Sweet so would I,
Yet I should kill thee with much cherishing:
Good night, good night.

ROMEO: Parting is such sweet sorrow,
That I shall say good night, till it be morrow. 10

JULIET: Sleep dwell upon thine eyes, peace in thy breast.

ROMEO: Would I were sleep and peace, so sweet to rest:
Hence will I to my ghostly Friar's close cell,
His help to crave, and my dear hap to tell.

Exeunt. 15

II.3

Enter Friar alone with a basket.

FRIAR LAURENCE: The grey-eyed morn smiles on the
frowning night,
Checkring the Eastern clouds with streaks of light: 20
And fleckled darkness like a drunkard reels,
From forth day's path, and Titan's burning wheels:
Now ere the sun advance his burning eye,
The day to cheer, and night's dank dew to dry,
I must up-fill this osier cage of ours, 25
With baleful weeds, and precious juiced flowers,
The earth that's Nature's mother is her tomb,
What is her burying grave, that is her womb:
And from her womb children of divers kind,
We sucking on her natural bosom find: 30

Many for many virtues excellent:
None but for some, and yet all different.
O mickle is the powerful grace that lies
In plants, herbs, stones, and their true qualities:
5 For nought so vile, that on the earth doth live,
But to the earth some special good doth give:
Nor aught so good but strain'd from that fair use,
Revolts from true birth, stumbling on abuse.
Virtue itself turns vice being misapplied,
10 And vice sometime by action dignified.

Enter Romeo.

Within the infant rind of this weak flower
Poison hath residence, and medicine power:
For this being smelt with that part, cheers each part,
15 Being tasted, slays all senses with the heart.
Two such opposed Kings encamp them still,
In man as well as herbs, grace and rude will:
And where the worser is predominant,
Full soon the canker death eats up that plant.
20 ROMEO: Good morrow father.
FRIAR LAURENCE: Benedicite.
What early tongue so soon saluteth me?
Young son, it argues a distempered head
So soon to bid good morrow to thy bed:
25 Care keeps his watch in every old man's eye,
And where care lodges, sleep will never lie:
But where unbruised youth with unstuff'd brain
Doth couch his limbs, there golden sleep doth reign.
Therefore thy earliness doth me assure,
30 Thou art up-rous'd with some distemperature:
Or if not so, then here I hit it right,
Our Romeo hath not been in bed to-night.

ROMEO: That last is true, the sweeter rest was mine.

FRIAR LAURENCE: God pardon sin, wast thou with Rosaline?

ROMEO: With Rosaline, my ghostly father no,
I have forgot that name, and that name's woe.   5

FRIAR LAURENCE: That's my good son, but where hast thou been then?

ROMEO: I'll tell thee ere thou ask it me again:
I have been feasting with mine enemy,
Where on a sudden one hath wounded me,   10
That's by me wounded: both our remedies
Within thy help and holy physic lies:
I bear no hatred blessed man: for lo
My intercession likewise steads my foe.

FRIAR LAURENCE: Be plain good son and homely in thy   15
drift,
Riddling confession, finds but riddling shrift.

ROMEO: Then plainly know my heart's dear love is set
On the fair daughter of rich Capulet:
As mine on hers, so hers is set on mine,   20
And all combin'd, save what thou must combine
By holy marriage, when and where, and how,
We met, we woo'd, and made exchange of vow,
I'll tell thee as we pass, but this I pray,
That thou consent to marry us to-day.   25

FRIAR LAURENCE: Holy Saint Francis what a change is
here?
Is Rosaline that thou didst love so dear,
So soon forsaken? Young men's love then lies
Not truly in their hearts, but in their eyes: 30
Jesu Maria, what a deal of brine
Hath wash'd thy sallow cheeks for Rosaline!

How much salt water thrown away in waste,
To season love, that of it doth not taste.
The Sun not yet thy sighs from heaven clears,
Thy old groans yet ring in mine ancient ears:

5   Lo here upon thy cheek the stain doth sit,
Of an old tear that is not wash'd off yet.
If e'er thou wast thyself, and these woes thine,
Thou and these woes were all for Rosaline.
And art thou chang'd, pronounce this sentence then,

10   Women may fall, when there's no strength in men.

ROMEO: Thou chid'st me oft for loving Rosaline.

FRIAR LAURENCE: For doting, not for loving, pupil mine.

ROMEO: And bad'st me bury love.

FRIAR LAURENCE: Not in a grave,

15   To lay one in, another out to have.

ROMEO: I pray thee chide me not, her I love now
Doth grace for grace, and love for love allow:
The other did not so.

FRIAR LAURENCE: O she knew well,

20   Thy love did read by rote, that could not spell:
But come young waverer, come go with me,
In one respect I'll thy assistant be:
For this alliance may so happy prove,
To turn your households' rancour to pure love.

25   ROMEO: O let us hence, I stand on sudden haste.

FRIAR LAURENCE: Wisely and slow, they stumble that
run fast.

Exeunt.

II. 4

Enter Benvolio and Mercutio.

MERCUTIO: Where the devil should this Romeo be? Came
he not home to-night?

BENVOLIO: Not to his father's, I spoke with his man.   5

MERCUTIO: Why that same pale hard-hearted wench, that
Rosaline,
Torments him so, that he will sure run mad.

BENVOLIO: Tybalt, the kinsman to old Capulet,
Hath sent a letter to his father's house.   10

MERCUTIO: A challenge on my life.

BENVOLIO: Romeo will answer it.

MERCUTIO: Any man that can write may answer a
letter.

BENVOLIO: Nay, he will answer the letter's master how   15
he dares, being dar'd.

MERCUTIO: Alas poor Romeo, he is already dead, stabb'd
with a white wench's black eye, run through the ear with
a love song, the very pin of his heart, cleft with the blind
bow-boy's butt-shaft, and is he a man to encounter Ty-   20
balt?

BENVOLIO: Why what is Tybalt?

MERCUTIO: More than Prince of Cats. O he 's the cour-
ageous captain of compliments: he fights as you sing
pricksong, keeps time, distance and proportion, he rests,   25
his minim rests, one two, and the third in your bosom:
the very butcher of a silk button, a duellist a duellist, a
gentleman of the very first house of the first and second
cause, ah the immortal passado, the punto reverso, the
hay.   30

BENVOLIO: The what?

MERCUTIO: The pox of such antic lisping affecting fantasies, these new tuners of accents: by Jesu, a very good
blade, a very tall man, a very good whore. Why is not
this a lamentable thing grandsire, that we should be thus
5 afflicted with these strange flies: these fashion-mongers,
these pardon-mes, who stand so much on the new form,
that they cannot sit at ease on the old bench. O their bons,
their bons.

Enter Romeo.

10 BENVOLIO: Here comes Romeo, here comes Romeo.
MERCUTIO: Without his roe, like a dried herring, O flesh,
flesh, how art thou fishified! Now is he for the numbers
that Petrarch flowed in: Laura to his Lady was a kitchen
wench, marry she had a better love to berhyme her: Dido
15 a dowdy, Cleopatra a gipsy, Helen and Hero, hildings
and harlots: Thisbe a grey eye or so, but not to the purpose. Signior Romeo, *bon jour,* there's a French saluta-
tion to your French slop: you gave us the counterfeit fairly last night.
20 ROMEO: Good morrow to you both, what counterfeit did
I give you?
MERCUTIO: The slip sir, the slip, can you not conceive?
ROMEO: Pardon good Mercutio, my business was great,
and in such a case as mine, a man may strain courtesy.
25 MERCUTIO: That's as much as to say, such a case as yours,
constrains a man to bow in the hams.
ROMEO: Meaning to court'sy.
MERCUTIO: Thou hast most kindly hit it.
ROMEO: A most courteous exposition.
30 MERCUTIO: Nay I am the very pink of courtesy.
ROMEO: Pink for flower.
MERCUTIO: Right.

ROMEO: Why then is my pump well flower'd.

MERCUTIO: Sure wit, follow me this jest, now till thou hast worn out thy pump, that when the single sole of it is worn, the jest may remain after the wearing, solely singular. 5

ROMEO: O single-sol'd jest, solely singular for the singleness.

MERCUTIO: Come between us good Benvolio, my wits faints.

ROMEO: Switch and spurs, switch and spurs, or I 'll cry a match. 10

MERCUTIO: Nay, if our wits run the wild-goose chase, I am done: for thou hast more of the wild-goose in one of thy wits, than I am sure I have in all my five. Was I with you there for the goose? 15

ROMEO: Thou wast never with me for anything, when thou wast not there for the goose.

MERCUTIO: I will bite thee by the ear for that jest.

ROMEO: Nay good goose bite not.

MERCUTIO: Thy wit is a very bitter sweeting, it is a most sharp sauce. 20

ROMEO: And it is not then well serv'd in to a sweet goose?

MERCUTIO: O here 's a wit of cheveril, that stretches from an inch narrow, to an ell broad.

ROMEO: I stretch it out for that word broad, which added to the goose, proves thee far and wide a broad goose. 25

MERCUTIO: Why is not this better now than groaning for love, now art thou sociable, now art thou Romeo: now art thou what thou art, by art as well as by nature, for this drivelling love is like a great natural that runs lolling up and down to hide his bauble in a hole. 30

BENVOLIO: Stop there, stop there.

MERCUTIO: Thou desirest me to stop in my tale against
the hair.

BENVOLIO: Thou wouldst else have made thy tale large.

MERCUTIO: O thou art deceiv'd, I would have made it
5   short, for I was come to the whole depth of my tale, and
meant indeed to occupy the argument no longer.

Enter Nurse and Peter her man.

ROMEO: Here 's goodly gear. A sail, a sail.

MERCUTIO: Two, two: a shirt and a smock.

10   NURSE: Peter!

PETER: Anon.

NURSE: My fan Peter.

MERCUTIO: Good Peter to hide her face, for her fan 's the
fairer face.

15   NURSE: God ye good morrow gentlemen.

MERCUTIO: God ye good den fair gentlewoman.

NURSE: Is it good den?

MERCUTIO: 'Tis no less I tell ye, for the bawdy hand of
the dial is now upon the prick of noon.

20   NURSE: Out upon you, what a man are you?

ROMEO: One, gentlewoman, that God hath made, himself
to mar.

NURSE: By my troth it is well said, for himself to mar,
quoth a'! Gentlemen can any of you tell me where I may
25   find the young Romeo?

ROMEO: I can tell you, but young Romeo will be older
when you have found him, than he was when you sought
him: I am the youngest of that name, for fault of a worse.

NURSE: You say well.

30   MERCUTIO: Yea is the worst well, very well took, i' faith,
wisely, wisely.

NURSE: If you be he sir, I desire some confidence with you.

BENVOLIO: She will indite him to some supper.

MERCUTIO: A bawd, a bawd, a bawd. So ho.

ROMEO: What hast thou found?

MERCUTIO: No hare sir, unless a hare sir in a lenten pie,
that is something stale and hoar ere it be spent.   5

⟨*He walks by them and sings.*⟩

An old hare hoar, and an old hare hoar
  Is very good meat in lent.
But a hare that is hoar, is too much for a score,
  When it hoars ere it be spent.   10

Romeo, will you come to your father's? We'll to dinner
thither.

ROMEO: I will follow you.

MERCUTIO: Farewell ancient Lady, farewell Lady, Lady,
Lady.   15

Exeunt.

NURSE: I pray you sir, what saucy merchant was this that
was so full of his ropery?

ROMEO: A gentleman Nurse, that loves to hear himself
talk, and will speak more in a minute, than he will stand   20
to in a month.

NURSE: And a' speak any thing against me, I'll take him
down, and a' were lustier than he is, and twenty such
Jacks: and if I cannot, I'll find those that shall: scurvy
knave, I am none of his flirt gills, I am none of his skains   25
mates, ⟨*she turns to Peter her man*⟩ and thou must stand by
too and suffer every knave to use me at his pleasure.

PETER: I saw no man use you at his pleasure: if I had, my
weapon should quickly have been out: I warrant you, I
dare draw as soon as another man, if I see occasion in a   30
good quarrel, and the law on my side.

NURSE: Now afore God, I am so vex'd, that every part

about me quivers, scurvy knave: pray you sir a word: and
as I told you, my young Lady bid me inquire you out,
what she bid me say, I will keep to myself: but first let
me tell ye, if ye should lead her in a fool's paradise, as they
5   say, it were a very gross kind of behaviour as they say:
for the gentlewoman is young: and therefore, if you
should deal double with her, truly it were an ill thing to
be offer'd to any gentlewoman, and very weak dealing.

ROMEO: Nurse, commend me to thy Lady and Mistress, I
10   protest unto thee.

NURSE: Good heart, and i' faith I will tell her as much:
Lord, Lord, she will be a joyful woman.

ROMEO: What wilt thou tell her Nurse? Thou dost not
mark me?

15   NURSE: I will tell her sir, that you do protest, which as I
take it, is a gentlemanlike offer.

ROMEO: Bid her devise
Some means to come to shrift this afternoon,
And there she shall at Friar Laurence' cell
20   Be shriv'd and married: here is for thy pains.

NURSE: No truly sir not a penny.

ROMEO: Go to, I say you shall.

NURSE: This afternoon sir, well she shall be there.

ROMEO: And stay good Nurse behind the Abbey wall,
25   Within this hour my man shall be with thee,
And bring thee cords made like a tackled stair,
Which to the high topgallant of my joy,
Must be my convoy in the secret night.
Farewell, be trusty, and I 'll quit thy pains:
30   Farewell, commend me to thy Mistress.

NURSE: Now God in heaven bless thee, hark you sir.

ROMEO: What say'st thou my dear Nurse?

NURSE: Is your man secret, did you ne'er hear say,
Two may keep counsel putting one away.

ROMEO: Warrant thee my man's as true as steel.

NURSE: Well sir, my Mistress is the sweetest Lady, Lord,
Lord, when 'twas a little prating thing. O there is a noble- 5
man in town one Paris, that would fain lay knife aboard:
but she good soul had as lieve see a toad, a very toad as
see him: I anger her sometimes, and tell her that Paris is
the properer man, but I 'll warrant you, when I say so,
she looks as pale as any clout in the versal world, doth not 10
rosemary and Romeo begin both with a letter?

ROMEO: Ay Nurse, what of that? Both with an R.

NURSE: A mocker that 's the dog's name, R is for the – no,
I know it begins with some other letter, and she hath the
prettiest sententious of it, of you and rosemary, that it 15
would do you good to hear it.

ROMEO: Commend me to thy Lady.

NURSE: Ay a thousand times: Peter.

PETER: Anon.

NURSE: Before and apace. 20

Exeunt.

II. 5

Enter Juliet.

JULIET: The clock struck nine when I did send the Nurse,
In half an hour she promised to return, 25
Perchance she cannot meet him; that 's not so:
Oh she is lame, love's heralds should be thoughts,
Which ten times faster glides than the Sun's beams,
Driving back shadows over louring hills.
Therefore do nimble pinion'd doves draw love, 30

And therefore hath the wind swift Cupid wings:
Now is the Sun upon the highmost hill
Of this day's journey, and from nine till twelve,
Is three long hours, yet she is not come.

5   Had she affections and warm youthful blood,
She would be as swift in motion as a ball,
My words would bandy her to my sweet love,
And his to me:
But old folks, many feign as they were dead,

10 Unwieldy, slow, heavy, and pale as lead.

Enter Nurse.

O God she comes, O honey Nurse what news?
Hast thou met with him? Send thy man away.

NURSE: Peter stay at the gate.

15 JULIET: Now good sweet Nurse, O Lord, why look'st
    thou sad?
Though news be sad, yet tell them merrily.
If good, thou shamest the music of sweet news,
By playing it to me, with so sour a face.

20 NURSE: I am a-weary, give me leave a while,
Fie how my bones ache, what a jaunce have I?

JULIET: I would thou hadst my bones, and I thy news:
Nay come I pray thee speak, good good Nurse speak.

NURSE: Jesu what haste, can you not stay a while?

25 Do you not see that I am out of breath?

JULIET: How art thou out of breath, when thou hast breath
To say to me, that thou art out of breath?
The excuse that thou dost make in this delay,
Is longer than the tale thou dost excuse.

30 Is thy news good or bad? Answer to that,
Say either, and I'll stay the circumstance:
Let me be satisfied, is 't good or bad?

NURSE: Well, you have made a simple choice, you know
not how to choose a man: Romeo, no not he though his
face be better than any man's, yet his leg excels all men's,
and for a hand and a foot and a body, though they be not
to be talk'd on, yet they are past compare: he is not the   5
flower of courtesy, but I 'll warrant him, as gentle as a
lamb: go thy ways wench, serve God. What have you
din'd at home?

JULIET: No, no. But all this did I know before.
What says he of our marriage, what of that?   10

NURSE: Lord how my head aches, what a head have I!
It beats as it would fall in twenty pieces.
My back o' t' other side, ah my back, my back:
Beshrew your heart for sending me about
To catch my death with jauncing up and down.   15

JULIET: I' faith I am sorry that thou art not well.
Sweet, sweet, sweet Nurse, tell me what says my love?

NURSE: Your love says like an honest gentleman, and a
courteous, and a kind, and a handsome, and I warrant a
virtuous, where is your mother?   20

JULIET: Where is my mother, why she is within,
Where should she be? How oddly thou repliest:
Your love says like an honest gentleman,
Where is your mother?

NURSE: O God's lady dear,   25
Are you so hot, marry come up I trow,
Is this the poultice for my aching bones:
Henceforward do your messages yourself.

JULIET: Here 's such a coil, come what says Romeo?

NURSE: Have you got leave to go to shrift to-day?   30

JULIET: I have.

NURSE: Then hie you hence to Friar Laurence' cell,

There stays a husband to make you a wife:
Now comes the wanton blood up in your cheeks,
They 'll be in scarlet straight at any news:
Hie you to Church, I must another way,
5   To fetch a ladder by the which your love
Must climb a bird's nest soon when it is dark:
I am the drudge, and toil in your delight,
But you shall bear the burthen soon at night.
Go I 'll to dinner, hie you to the cell.
10 JULIET: Hie to high fortune, honest Nurse farewell.

Exeunt.

II. 6

Enter Friar and Romeo.

FRIAR LAURENCE: So smile the heavens upon this holy
15   act,
That after hours with sorrow chide us not.
ROMEO: Amen, amen, but come what sorrow can,
It cannot countervail the exchange of joy
That one short minute gives me in her sight:
20   Do thou but close our hands with holy words,
Then love-devouring death do what he dare,
It is enough I may but call her mine.
FRIAR LAURENCE: These violent delights have violent
ends,
25   And in their triumph die like fire and powder:
Which as they kiss consume. The sweetest honey
Is loathsome in his own deliciousness,
And in the taste confounds the appetite.
Therefore love moderately, long love doth so,
30   Too swift arrives, as tardy as too slow.

⟨*Enter Juliet somewhat fast, and embraceth Romeo.*⟩
Here comes the Lady. Oh so light a foot
Will ne'er wear out the everlasting flint,
A lover may bestride the gossamers,
That idles in the wanton summer air,⁣   5
And yet not fall, so light is vanity.

JULIET: Good even to my ghostly confessor.

FRIAR LAURENCE: Romeo shall thank thee daughter for
    us both.

JULIET: As much to him, else is his thanks too much.   10

ROMEO: Ah Juliet, if the measure of thy joy
    Be heap'd like mine, and that thy skill be more
    To blazon it, then sweeten with thy breath
    This neighbour air, and let rich music's tongue
    Unfold the imagin'd happiness that both   15
    Receive in either, by this dear encounter.

JULIET: Conceit more rich in matter than in words,
    Brags of his substance, not of ornament:
    They are but beggars that can count their worth,
    But my true love is grown to such excess,   20
    I cannot sum up sum of half my wealth.

FRIAR LAURENCE: Come, come with me, and we will
    make short work.
For by your leaves, you shall not stay alone,
Till holy Church incorporate two in one.   25
             Exeunt.

III. 1

Enter Mercutio, Benvolio, and Men.

BENVOLIO: I pray thee good Mercutio let's retire,
    The day is hot, the Capulets abroad: 30

And if we meet we shall not 'scape a brawl,
For now these hot days, is the mad blood stirring.

MERCUTIO: Thou art like one of these fellows, that when
he enters the confines of a tavern, claps me his sword on
the table, and says, God send me no need of thee: and by
the operation of the second cup, draws him on the drawer, when indeed there is no need.

BENVOLIO: Am I like such a fellow?

MERCUTIO: Come, come, thou art as hot a Jack in thy
mood as any in Italy: and as soon mov'd to be moody,
and as soon moody to be mov'd.

BENVOLIO: And what to?

MERCUTIO: Nay and there were two such, we should have
none shortly, for one would kill the other: thou, why
thou wilt quarrel with a man that hath a hair more, or a
hair less in his beard, than thou hast: thou wilt quarrel
with a man for cracking nuts, having no other reason, but
because thou hast hazel eyes: what eye, but such an eye
would spy out such a quarrel? Thy head is as full of quarrels, as an egg is full of meat, and yet thy head hath been
beaten as addle as an egg for quarreling: though hast quarrell'd with a man for coughing in the street, because he
hath wakened thy dog that hath lain asleep in the sun.
Didst thou not fall out with a tailor for wearing his new
doublet before Easter, with another for tying his new
shoes with old riband, and yet thou wilt tutor me from
quarrelling?

BENVOLIO: And I were so apt to quarrel as thou art, any
man should buy the fee-simple of my life for an hour and
a quarter.

MERCUTIO: The fee-simple, O simple.

Enter Tybalt and others.

BENVOLIO: By my head here comes the Capulets.

MERCUTIO: By my heel I care not.

TYBALT: Follow me close, for I will speak to them.
Gentlemen, good den, a word with one of you.

MERCUTIO: And but one word with one of us, couple it   5
with something, make it a word and a blow.

TYBALT: You shall find me apt enough to that sir, and you
will give me occasion.

MERCUTIO: Could you not take some occasion without
giving?   10

TYBALT: Mercutio, thou consortest with Romeo.

MERCUTIO: Consort, what dost thou make us minstrels?
And thou make minstrels of us, look to hear nothing but
discords: here's my fiddlestick, here's that shall make
you dance: 'zounds consort.   15

BENVOLIO: We talk here in the public haunt of men:
Either withdraw unto some private place,
Or reason coldly of your grievances:
Or else depart, here all eyes gaze on us.

MERCUTIO: Men's eyes were made to look, and let them   20
gaze.
I will not budge for no man's pleasure I.
                Enter Romeo.

TYBALT: Well peace be with you sir, here comes my
man.   25

MERCUTIO: But I'll be hang'd sir if he wear your livery:
Marry go before to field, he'll be your follower,
Your worship in that sense may call him man.

TYBALT: Romeo, the love I bear thee, can afford
No better term than this thou art a villain.   30

ROMEO: Tybalt, the reason that I have to love thee,
Doth much excuse the appertaining rage

To such a greeting: villain am I none.
Therefore farewell, I see thou know'st me not.

TYBALT: Boy, this shall not excuse the injuries
That thou hast done me, therefore turn and draw.

5   ROMEO: I do protest I never injur'd thee,
But love thee better than thou canst devise:
Till thou shalt know the reason of my love,
And so good Capulet, which name I tender
As dearly as mine own, be satisfied.

10   MERCUTIO: O calm, dishonourable, vile submission:
Alla stoccata carries it away.
Tybalt, you rat-catcher, will you walk?

TYBALT: What wouldst thou have with me?

MERCUTIO: Good King of Cats, nothing but one of your
15   nine lives, that I mean to make bold withal, and as you
shall use me hereafter dry-beat the rest of the eight. Will
you pluck your sword out of his pilcher by the ears?
Make haste, lest mine be about your ears ere it be out.

TYBALT: I am for you.

20   ROMEO: Gentle Mercutio, put thy rapier up.

MERCUTIO: Come sir, your passado.

ROMEO: Draw Benvolio, beat down their weapons:
Gentlemen, for shame forbear this outrage,
Tybalt, Mercutio, the Prince expressly hath
25   Forbid this bandying in Verona streets,
Hold Tybalt, good Mercutio.

⟨*Tybalt under Romeo's arm thrusts Mercutio in; and flies.*⟩

MERCUTIO: I am hurt.
A plague o' both houses, I am sped:
30   Is he gone and hath nothing?

BENVOLIO: What art thou hurt?

MERCUTIO: Ay, ay, a scratch, a scratch, marry 'tis enough.

Where is my page? Go villain, fetch a surgeon.
Exit Page.

ROMEO: Courage man, the hurt cannot be much.

MERCUTIO: No 'tis not so deep as a well, nor so wide as a
churchdoor, but 'tis enough, 'twill serve: ask for me to- 5
morrow, and you shall find me a grave man. I am pep-
pered I warrant, for this world, a plague a' both your
houses, 'zounds, a dog, a rat, a mouse, a cat, to scratch a
man to death: a braggart, a rogue a villain, that fights by
the book of arithmetic, why the devil came you between 10
us? I was hurt under your arm.

ROMEO: I thought all for the best.

MERCUTIO: Help me into some house Benvolio,
Or I shall faint, a plague a' both your houses,
They have made worms' meat of me, 15
I have it, and soundly, to your houses.
Exeunt Mercutio and Benvolio.

ROMEO: This gentleman the Prince's near ally,
My very friend hath got this mortal hurt
In my behalf, my reputation stain'd 20
With Tybalt's slander, Tybalt that an hour
Hath been my cousin: O sweet Juliet,
Thy beauty hath made me effeminate,
And in my temper soften'd valour's steel.
Enter Benvolio. 25

BENVOLIO: O Romeo, Romeo, brave Mercutio is dead,
That gallant spirit hath aspir'd the clouds,
Which too untimely here did scorn the earth.

ROMEO: This day's black fate, on moe days doth depend;
This but begins, the woe others must end. 30
Enter Tybalt.

BENVOLIO: Here comes the furious Tybalt back again.

ROMEO: He gone in triumph, and Mercutio slain?
Away to heaven, respective lenity,
And fire and fury, be my conduct now.
Now Tybalt take the villain back again,
5   That late thou gav'st me, for Mercutio's soul
Is but a little way above our heads,
Staying for thine to keep him company:
Either thou or I, or both, must go with him.

TYBALT: Thou wretched boy that didst consort him here,
10   Shalt with him hence.

ROMEO: This shall determine that.

They fight. Tybalt falls.

BENVOLIO: Romeo, away be gone:
The citizens are up, and Tybalt slain,
15   Stand not amaz'd, the Prince will doom thee death,
If thou art taken, hence be gone away.

ROMEO: O I am fortune's fool.

BENVOLIO: Why dost thou stay?

Exit Romeo.
20   *Enter Citizens.*

CITIZEN: Which way ran he that kill'd Mercutio?
Tybalt that murtherer, which way ran he?

BENVOLIO: There lies that Tybalt.

CITIZEN: Up sir, go with me:
25   I charge thee in the Prince's name obey.

Enter Prince, old Montague, Capulet, their Wives, and all.

PRINCE: Where are the vile beginners of this fray?

BENVOLIO: O noble Prince, I can discover all
The unlucky manage of this fatal brawl:
30   There lies the man slain by young Romeo,
That slew thy kinsman, brave Mercutio.

LADY CAPULET: Tybalt, my cousin, O my brother's child,

O Prince, O cousin, husband, O the blood is spilt
Of my dear kinsman, Prince as thou art true,
For blood of ours, shed blood of Montague.
O cousin, cousin.

PRINCE: Benvolio, who began this bloody fray?   5

BENVOLIO: Tybalt here slain, whom Romeo's hand did
    slay,
Romeo that spake him fair, bid him bethink
How nice the quarrel was, and urg'd withal
Your high displeasure: all this uttered,   10
With gentle breath, calm look, knees humbly bow'd
Could not take truce with the unruly spleen
Of Tybalt deaf to peace, but that he tilts
With piercing steel at bold Mercutio's breast,
Who all as hot, turns deadly point to point,   15
And with a martial scorn, with one hand beats
Cold death aside, and with the other sends
It back to Tybalt, whose dexterity
Retorts it: Romeo he cries aloud,
Hold friends, friends part, and swifter than his tongue,   20
His agile arm beats down their fatal points,
And 'twixt them rushes, underneath whose arm,
An envious thrust from Tybalt, hit the life
Of stout Mercutio, and then Tybalt fled,
But by and by comes back to Romeo,   25
Who had but newly entertain'd revenge,
And to 't they go like lightning, for ere I
Could draw to part them, was stout Tybalt slain:
And as he fell, did Romeo turn and fly:
This is the truth, or let Benvolio die.   30

LADY CAPULET: He is a kinsman to the Montague,
Affection makes him false, he speaks not true:

Some twenty of them fought in this black strife,
And all those twenty could but kill one life.
I beg for justice, which thou Prince must give:
Romeo slew Tybalt, Romeo must not live.

5 PRINCE: Romeo slew him, he slew Mercutio,
Who now the price of his dear blood doth owe.

MONTAGUE: Not Romeo Prince, he was Mercutio's friend,
His fault concludes, but what the law should end,

10 The life of Tybalt.

PRINCE: And for that offence,
Immediately we do exile him hence:
I have an interest in your hate's proceeding:
My blood for your rude brawls doth lie a-bleeding.

15 But I'll amerce you with so strong a fine,
That you shall all repent the loss of mine.
I will be deaf to pleading and excuses,
Nor tears, nor prayers shall purchase out abuses.
Therefore use none, let Romeo hence in haste,

20 Else when he 's found, that hour is his last.
Bear hence this body, and attend our will,
Mercy but murders, pardoning those that kill.

Exeunt.

III. 2

25 *Enter Juliet alone.*

JULIET: Gallop apace, you fiery-footed steeds,
Towards Phœbus' lodging, such a waggoner
As Phaethon would whip you to the west,
And bring in cloudy night immediately.

Spread thy close curtain love-performing night,
That runaways eyes may wink, and Romeo
Leap to these arms, untalk'd of and unseen,
Lovers can see to do their amorous rites,
By their own beauties, or if love be blind,   5
It best agrees with night: come civil night,
Thou sober-suited matron all in black,
And learn me how to lose a winning match,
Play'd for a pair of stainless maidenhoods.
Hood my unmann'd blood baiting in my cheeks,   10
With thy black mantle, till strange love grow bold,
Think true love acted simple modesty:
Come night, come Romeo, come thou day in night,
For thou wilt lie upon the wings of night,
Whiter than new snow on a raven's back: 15
Come gentle night, come loving black-brow'd night,
Give me my Romeo, and when he shall die,
Take him and cut him out in little stars,
And he will make the face of heaven so fine,
That all the world will be in love with night,   20
And pay no worship to the garish Sun.
O I have bought the mansion of a love,
But not possess'd it, and though I am sold,
Not yet enjoy'd, so tedious is this day,
As is the night before some festival,   25
To an impatient child that hath new robes
And may not wear them. O here comes my Nurse:
⟨*Enter Nurse wringing her hands, with the ladder of
cords in her lap.*⟩
And she brings news, and every tongue that speaks   30
But Romeo's name, speaks heavenly eloquence.
Now Nurse, what news? What hast thou there, the cords

That Romeo bid thee fetch?

NURSE: Ay, ay, the cords.

JULIET: Ay me what news? Why dost thou wring thy
   hands?

5 NURSE: Ah well-a-day, he 's dead, he 's dead, he 's dead,
   We are undone Lady, we are undone.
   Alack the day, he's gone, he's kill'd, he's dead.

JULIET: Can heaven be so envious?

NURSE: Romeo can,

10   Though heaven cannot. O Romeo, Romeo,
   Who ever would have thought it Romeo?

JULIET: What devil art thou that dost torment me thus?
   This torture should be roar'd in dismal hell,
   Hath Romeo slain himself? Say thou but ay,

15   And that bare vowel ay shall poison more
   Than the death-darting eye of cockatrice.
   I am not I, if there be such an ay,
   Or those eyes shut, that make thee answer ay:
   If he be slain say ay, or if not, no:

20   Brief sounds, determine of my weal or woe.

NURSE: I saw the wound, I saw it with mine eyes,
   God save the mark, here on his manly breast,
   A piteous corse, a bloody piteous corse,
   Pale, pale as ashes, all bedaub'd in blood,

25   All in gore blood, I sounded at the sight.

JULIET: O break my heart, poor bankrout break at once,
   To prison eyes, ne'er look on liberty.
   Vile earth to earth resign, end motion here,
   And thou and Romeo press one heavy bier.

30 NURSE: O Tybalt, Tybalt, the best friend I had,
   O courteous Tybalt, honest gentleman,
   That ever I should live to see thee dead.

JULIET: What storm is this that blows so contrary?
    Is Romeo slaughter'd? and is Tybalt dead?
    My dearest cousin, and my dearer Lord.
    Then dreadful trumpet sound the general doom,
    For who is living, if those two are gone?   5
NURSE: Tybalt is gone and Romeo banished,
    Romeo that kill'd him, he is banished.
JULIET: O God, did Romeo's hand shed Tybalt's blood?
NURSE: It did, it did, alas the day, it did.
JULIET: O serpent heart, hid with a flowering face,   10
    Did ever dragon keep so fair a cave?
    Beautiful tyrant, fiend angelical:
    Dove-feather'd raven, wolvish-ravening lamb,
    Despised substance of divinest show:
    Just opposite to what thou justly seem'st,   15
    A damned saint, an honourable villain:
    O nature what hadst thou to do in hell
    When thou didst bower the spirit of a fiend,
    In mortal paradise of such sweet flesh?
    Was ever book containing such vile matter   20
    So fairly bound? O that deceit should dwell
    In such a gorgeous Palace.
NURSE: There 's no trust,
    No faith, no honesty in men, all perjur'd,
    All forsworn, all naught, all dissemblers.   25
    Ah where 's my man? Give me some aqua vitae:
    These griefs, these woes, these sorrows make me old,
    Shame come to Romeo.
JULIET: Blister'd be thy tongue
    For such a wish, he was not born to shame: 30
    Upon his brow shame is asham'd to sit:
    For 'tis a throne where honour may be crown'd

Sole monarch of the universal earth.
O what a beast was I to chide at him!

NURSE: Will you speak well of him that kill'd your cousin?

5 JULIET: Shall I speak ill of him that is my husband?
Ah poor my Lord, what tongue shall smooth thy name,
When I thy three-hours wife have mangled it?
But wherefore villain didst thou kill my cousin?
That villain cousin would have kill'd my husband:
10 Back foolish tears, back to your native spring,
Your tributary drops belong to woe,
Which you mistaking offer up to joy:
My husband lives that Tybalt would have slain,
And Tybalt's dead that would have slain my husband:
15 All this is comfort, wherefore weep I then?
Some word there was, worser than Tybalt's death
That murder'd me, I would forget it fain,
But Oh it presses to my memory,
Like damned guilty deeds to sinners' minds,
20 Tybalt is dead and Romeo banished:
That banished, that one word banished,
Hath slain ten thousand Tybalts: Tybalt's death
Was woe enough if it had ended there:
Or if sour woe delights in fellowship,
25 And needly will be rank'd with other griefs,
Why follow'd not when she said Tybalt's dead,
Thy father or thy mother, nay or both,
Which modern lamentation might have mov'd.
But with a rearward following Tybalt's death,
30 Romeo is banished: to speak that word,
Is father, mother, Tybalt, Romeo, Juliet,
All slain, all dead: Romeo is banished,

There is no end, no limit, measure bound,
In that word's death, no words can that woe sound.
Where is my father and my mother Nurse?
NURSE: Weeping and wailing over Tybalt's corse,
Will you go to them? I will bring you thither.   5
JULIET: Wash they his wounds with tears? Mine shall be
    spent,
When theirs are dry, for Romeo's banishment.
Take up those cords, poor ropes you are beguil'd,
Both you and I for Romeo is exil'd: 10
He made you for a highway to my bed,
But I a maid, die maiden widowed.
Come cords, come Nurse, I'll to my wedding-bed,
And death not Romeo, take my maidenhead.
NURSE: Hie to your chamber, I'll find Romeo   15
To comfort you, I wot well where he is:
Hark ye, your Romeo will be here at night,
I'll to him, he is hid at Laurence' cell.
JULIET: O find him, give this ring to my true knight,
And bid him come, to take his last farewell.   20
                        Exeunt.

III. 3

Enter Friar Laurence and Romeo.

FRIAR LAURENCE: Romeo come forth, come forth thou
    fearful man,   25
Affliction is enamour'd of thy parts:
And thou art wedded to calamity.
ROMEO: Father what news? What is the Prince's doom?
What sorrow craves acquaintance at my hand,
That I yet know not?   30

FRIAR LAURENCE: Too familiar
Is my dear son with such sour company:
I bring thee tidings of the Prince's doom.
ROMEO: What less than doomsday is the Prince's doom?
5 FRIAR LAURENCE: A gentler judgement vanish'd from his
lips,
Not body's death, but body's banishment.
ROMEO: Ha, banishment? Be merciful, say death:
For exile hath more terror in his look,
10 Much more than death, do not say banishment.
FRIAR LAURENCE: Hence from Verona art thou banish-
ed:
Be patient, for the world is broad and wide.
ROMEO: There is no world without Verona walls,
15 But purgatory, torture, hell itself:
Hence banished, is banish'd from the world.
And world's exile is death. Then banished,
Is death, mis-term'd, calling death banished,
Thou cut'st my head off with a golden axe,
20 And smilest upon the stroke that murders me.
FRIAR LAURENCE: O deadly sin, O rude unthankfulness,
Thy fault our law calls death, but the kind Prince
Taking thy part, hath rush'd aside the law,
And turn'd that black word death to banishment.
25 This is dear mercy, and thou seest it not.
ROMEO: 'Tis torture and not mercy, heaven is here
Where Juliet lives, and every cat and dog,
And little mouse, every unworthy thing
Live here in heaven, and may look on her,
30 But Romeo may not. More validity,
More honourable state, more courtship lives
In carrion-flies, than Romeo: they may seize

On the white wonder of dear Juliet's hand,
And steal immortal blessing from her lips,
Who even in pure vestal modesty
Still blush, as thinking their own kisses sin.
This may flies do, when I from this must fly,   5
And say'st thou yet, that exile is not death?
But Romeo may not, he is banished.
Flies may do this, but I from this must fly:
They are free men, but I am banished.
Hadst thou no poison mix'd, no sharp-ground knife,   10
No sudden mean of death, though ne'er so mean,
But banished to kill me? Banished?
O Friar, the damned use that word in hell:
Howling attends it, how hadst thou the heart
Being a divine, a ghostly confessor,   15
A sin-absolver, and my friend profess'd,
To mangle me with that word banished?

FRIAR LAURENCE: Thou fond mad man, hear me a little
  speak.

ROMEO: O thou wilt speak again of banishment.   20

FRIAR LAURENCE: I 'll give thee armour to keep off that
  word,
  Adversity's sweet milk, Philosophy,
  To comfort thee though thou art banished.

ROMEO: Yet banished? Hang up philosophy,   25
  Unless philosophy can make a Juliet,
  Displant a town, reverse a Prince's doom,
  It helps not, it prevails not, talk no more.

FRIAR LAURENCE: O then I see, that madmen have no
  ears.   30

ROMEO: How should they, when that wise men have no
  eyes?

FRIAR LAURENCE: Let me dispute with thee of thy estate
ROMEO: Thou canst not speak of that thou dost not feel.·
　　Wert thou as young as I, Juliet thy love,
　　An hour but married, Tybalt murdered,
5　　Doting like me, and like me banished,
　　Then mightst thou speak,
　　Then mightst thou tear thy hair,
　　And fall upon the ground as I do now,
　　Taking the measure of an unmade grave.
10　　　　　　　　　⟨*Nurse knocks.*⟩
FRIAR LAURENCE: Arise, one knocks, good Romeo hide
　　thyself.
ROMEO: Not I, unless the breath of heart-sick groans
　　Mist-like infold me from the search of eyes.
15　　　　　　　　　⟨*She knocks again.*⟩
FRIAR LAURENCE: Hark how they knock: (who's there?)
　　Romeo arise,
　　Thou wilt be taken, stay awhile, stand up.
　　　　　　　　　　　Knock.
20　　Run to my study: by and by: God's will
　　What simpleness is this? I come, I come.
　　　　　　　　　　　Knock.
　　Who knocks so hard? Whence come you? What's your
　　will?
25 NURSE *within*: Let me come in, and you shall know my
　　errand:
　　I come from Lady Juliet.
FRIAR LAURENCE: Welcome then.
　　　　　　　　　　Enter Nurse.
30 NURSE: O holy Friar, O tell me holy Friar,
　　Where's my Lady's Lord. Where's Romeo?
FRIAR LAURENCE: There on the ground,

With his own tears made drunk.

NURSE: O he is even in my Mistress' case,
Just in her case. O woeful sympathy:
Piteous predicament, even so lies she,
Blubbering and weeping, weeping and blubbering,   5
Stand up, stand up, stand and you be a man,
For Juliet's sake, for her sake rise and stand:
Why should you fall into so deep an O?

⟨*He rises.*⟩

ROMEO: Nurse.   10

NURSE: Ah sir, ah sir, death's the end of all.

ROMEO: Spak'st thou of Juliet? How is it with her?
Doth she not think me an old murtherer,
Now I have stain'd the childhood of our joy,
With blood removed but little from her own?   15
Where is she? And how doth she? And what says
My conceal'd Lady to our cancell'd love?

NURSE: Oh she says nothing sir, but weeps and weeps,
And now falls on her bed, and then starts up,
And Tybalt calls, and then on Romeo cries,   20
And then down falls again.

ROMEO: As if that name
Shot from the deadly level of a gun
Did murther her, as that name's cursed hand
Murder'd her kinsman. Oh tell me Friar, tell me,   25
In what vile part of this anatomy
Doth my name lodge? Tell me that I may sack
The hateful mansion.

⟨*He offers to stab himself, and the Nurse snatches the
dagger away.*   30

NURSE: Ah?⟩

FRIAR LAURENCE: Hold thy desperate hand:

Art thou a man? Thy form cries out thou art:
Thy tears are womanish, thy wild acts denote
The unreasonable fury of a beast.
Unseemly woman in a seeming man,
5   And ill-beseeming beast in seeming both,
Thou hast amaz'd me. By my holy order,
I thought thy disposition better temper'd.
Hast thou slain Tybalt? Wilt thou slay thyself?
And slay thy Lady, that in thy life lives,
10 By doing damned hate upon thyself?
Why rail'st thou on thy birth? The heaven and earth?
Since birth, and heaven, and earth all three do meet
In thee at once, which thou at once wouldst lose.
Fie, fie, thou shamest thy shape, thy love, thy wit,
15 Which like a usurer abound'st in all:
And usest none in that true use indeed,
Which should bedeck thy shape, thy love, thy wit:
Thy noble shape is but a form of wax,
Digressing from the valour of a man,
20 Thy dear love sworn but hollow perjury,
Killing that love which thou hast vow'd to cherish,
Thy wit, that ornament, to shape and love,
Mis-shapen in the conduct of them both:
Like powder in a skilless soldier's flask,
25 Is set a-fire by thine own ignorance,
And thou dismember'd with thine own defence.
What rouse thee man, thy Juliet is alive,
For whose dear sake thou wast but lately dead.
There art thou happy: Tybalt would kill thee,
30 But thou slew'st Tybalt: there art thou happy.
The law that threaten'd death becomes thy friend,
And turns it to exile, there art thou happy.

A pack of blessings light upon thy back,
Happiness courts thee in her best array,
But like a misbehav'd and sullen wench,
Thou puttest up thy fortune and thy love:
Take heed, take heed, for such die miserable.   5
Go get thee to thy love as was decreed,
Ascend her chamber, hence and comfort her:
But look thou stay not till the watch be set,
For then thou canst not pass to Mantua,
Where thou shalt live till we can find a time   10
To blaze your marriage, reconcile your friends,
Beg pardon of the Prince, and call thee back,
With twenty hundred thousand times more joy
Than thou went'st forth in lamentation.
Go before Nurse, commend me to thy Lady,   15
And bid her hasten all the house to bed,
Which heavy sorrow makes them apt unto.
Romeo is coming.
NURSE: O Lord, I could have stay'd here all the night,
To hear good counsel, O what learning is: 20
My Lord, I 'll tell my Lady you will come.
ROMEO: Do so, and bid my sweet prepare to chide.
          ⟨*Nurse offers to go in and turns again.*⟩
NURSE: Here sir, a ring she bid me give you sir:
Hie you, make haste, for it grows very late.   25
          Exit.
ROMEO: How well my comfort is reviv'd by this.
FRIAR LAURENCE: Go hence, good night, and here stands
     all your state:
Either be gone before the watch be set,   30
Or by the break of day disguis'd from hence:
Sojourn in Mantua, I 'll find out your man,

And he shall signify from time to time,
Every good hap to you that chances here:
Give me thy hand, 'tis late, farewell, good night.
ROMEO: But that a joy past joy calls out on me,
5   It were a grief, so brief to part with thee:
Farewell.

Exeunt.

III. 4

Enter old Capulet, his wife and Paris.

10 CAPULET: Things have fall'n out sir so unluckily,
That we have had no time to move our daughter:
Look you, she lov'd her kinsman Tybalt dearly,
And so did I. Well we were born to die.
'Tis very late, she 'll not come down to-night:
15   I promise you, but for your company,
I would have been a-bed an hour ago.
PARIS: These times of woe afford no times to woo:
Madam good night, commend me to your daughter.
LADY CAPULET: I will, and know her mind early to-mor-
20   row,
To night she 's mew'd up to her heaviness.
⟨*Paris offers to go in, and Capulet calls him again.*⟩
CAPULET: Sir Paris, I will make a desperate tender
Of my child's love: I think she will be rul'd
25   In all respects by me: nay more, I doubt it not.
Wife, go you to her ere you go to bed,
Acquaint her here, of my son Paris' love,
And bid her, mark you me? on Wednesday next.
But soft, what day is this?
30 PARIS: Monday my Lord.
CAPULET: Monday, ha ha, well Wednesday is too soon,

A' Thursday let it be, a' Thursday tell her,
She shall be married to this noble Earl:
Will you be ready? Do you like this haste?
We 'll keep no great ado, a friend or two,
For hark you, Tybalt being slain so late,   5
It may be thought we held him carelessly
Being our kinsman, if we revel much:
Therefore we 'll have some half a dozen friends,
And there an end, but what say you to Thursday?
PARIS: My Lord, I would that Thursday were to-morrow.   10
CAPULET: Well get you gone, a' Thursday be it then:
Go you to Juliet ere you go to bed,
Prepare her wife, against this wedding day.
Farewell my Lord, light to my chamber ho,
Afore me, it is so very late   15
That we may call it early by and by,
Good night.
                            Exeunt.

III. 5

Enter Romeo and Juliet aloft ⟨at the window.⟩   20
JULIET: Wilt thou be gone? It is not yet near day:
It was the nightingale, and not the lark,
That pierc'd the fearful hollow of thine ear,
Nightly she sings on yond pomegranate tree,
Believe me love, it was the nightingale.   25
ROMEO: It was the lark, the herald of the morn:
No nightingale: look love what envious streaks
Do lace the severing clouds in yonder East:
Night's candles are burnt out, and jocund day
Stands tiptoe on the misty mountain tops,   30
I must be gone and live, or stay and die.

JULIET: Yond light is not daylight, I know it I:
It is some meteor that the Sun exhales,
To be to thee this night a torch-bearer,
And light thee on thy way to Mantua.
5   Therefore stay yet, thou needs not to be gone.
ROMEO: Let me be ta'en, let me be put to death,
I am content, so thou wilt have it so.
I'll say yon grey is not the morning's eye,
'Tis but the pale reflex of Cynthia's brow.
10   Nor that is not the lark whose notes do beat
The vaulty heaven so high above our heads,
I have more care to stay, than will to go:
Come death and welcome, Juliet wills it so.
How is't my soul? Let 's talk, it is not day.
15 JULIET: It is, it is, hie hence be gone away:
It is the lark that sings so out of tune,
Straining harsh discords, and unpleasing sharps.
Some say, the lark makes sweet division:
This doth not so: for she divideth us.
20   Some say the lark and loathed toad change eyes,
Oh now I would they had chang'd voices too:
Since arm from arm that voice doth us affray,
Hunting thee hence, with hunts-up to the day.
So now be gone, more light and light it grows.
25 ROMEO: More light and light, more dark and dark our
        woes.

Enter Nurse.

NURSE: Madam.
JULIET: Nurse.
30 NURSE: Your Lady mother is coming to your chamber,
The day is broke, be wary, look about.
Exit.

JULIET: Then window let day in, and let life out.
ROMEO: Farewell, farewell, one kiss and I'll descend.
                    ⟨*He goeth down.*⟩
JULIET: Art thou gone so love, Lord, ay husband, friend,
  I must hear from thee every day in the hour,   5
  For in a minute there are many days,
  O by this count I shall be much in years,
  Ere I again behold my Romeo.
ROMEO: Farewell:
  I will omit no opportunity,   10
  That may convey my greetings love to thee.
JULIET: O think'st thou we shall ever meet again?
ROMEO: I doubt it not, and all these woes shall serve
  For sweet discourses in our times to come.
JULIET: O God, I have an ill-divining soul,   15
  Methinks I see thee now, thou art so low,
  As one dead in the bottom of a tomb,
  Either my eyesight fails, or thou look'st pale.
ROMEO: And trust me love, in my eye so do you:
  Dry sorrow drinks our blood. Adieu, adieu.   20
                    Exit.
JULIET: O Fortune, Fortune, all men call thee fickle,
  If thou art fickle, what dost thou with him
  That is renown'd for faith? Be fickle Fortune:
  For then I hope thou wilt not keep him long,   25
  But send him back.
            ⟨*She goeth down from the window.*⟩
                Enter Lady Capulet.
LADY CAPULET: Ho daughter, are you up?
JULIET: Who is 't that calls? It is my Lady mother.   30
  Is she not down so late or up so early?
  What unaccustom'd cause procures her hither?

LADY CAPULET: Why how now Juliet?

JULIET: Madam I am not well.

LADY CAPULET: Evermore weeping for your cousin's
death?

5   What wilt thou wash him from his grave with tears?
And if thou couldst, thou couldst not make him live:
Therefore have done, some grief shows much of love,
But much of grief shows still some want of wit.

JULIET: Yet let me weep, for such a feeling loss.

10   LADY CAPULET: So shall you feel the loss, but not the
friend
Which you weep for.

JULIET: Feeling so the loss,
I cannot choose but ever weep the friend.

15   LADY CAPULET: Well girl, thou weep'st not so much for
his death,
As that the villain lives which slaughter'd him.

JULIET: What villain Madam?

LADY CAPULET: That same villain Romeo.

20   JULIET: Villain and he be many miles asunder:
God pardon him, I do with all my heart:
And yet no man like he, doth grieve my heart.

LADY CAPULET: That is because the traitor murderer lives.

JULIET: Ay Madam from the reach of these my hands:

25   Would none but I might venge my cousin's death.

LADY CAPULET: We will have vengeance for it, fear thou
not.
Then weep no more, I'll send to one in Mantua,
Where that same banish'd runagate doth live,

30   Shall give him such an unaccustom'd dram,
That he shall soon keep Tybalt company:
And then I hope thou wilt be satisfied.

JULIET: Indeed I never shall be satisfied
    With Romeo, till I behold him. Dead
    Is my poor heart so for a kinsman vex'd:
    Madam if you could find out but a man
    To bear a poison, I would temper it,   5
    That Romeo should upon receipt thereof,
    Soon sleep in quiet. Oh how my heart abhors
    To hear him nam'd and cannot come to him,
    To wreak the love I bore my cousin,
    Upon his body that hath slaughter'd him.   10
LADY CAPULET: Find thou the means, and I'll find such a
    man,
    But now I'll tell thee joyful tidings girl.
JULIET: And joy comes well in such a needy time,
    What are they, I beseech your Ladyship.   15
LADY CAPULET: Well, well, thou hast a careful father,
    child,
    One who to put thee from thy heaviness,
    Hath sorted out a sudden day of joy,
    That thou expect'st not, nor I look'd not for.   20
JULIET: Madam in happy time, what day is that?
LADY CAPULET: Marry my child, early next Thursday
    morn,
    The gallant young, and noble gentleman,
    The County Paris at Saint Peter's Church,   25
    Shall happily make thee there a joyful bride.
JULIET: Now by Saint Peter's Church, and Peter too,
    He shall not make me there a joyful bride.
    I wonder at this haste, that I must wed
    Ere he that should be husband comes to woo: 30
    I pray you tell my Lord and father Madam,
    I will not marry yet, and when I do, I swear

It shall be Romeo, whom you know I hate,
Rather than Paris, these are news indeed.

LADY CAPULET: Here comes your father, tell him so yourself:

5   And see how he will take it at your hands.

Enter Capulet and Nurse.

CAPULET: When the Sun sets, the earth doth drizzle
dew,
But for the sunset of my brother's son,

10   It rains downright.
How now a conduit girl, what still in tears
Evermore showering in one little body?
Thou counterfeit'st a bark, a sea, a wind:
For still thy eyes, which I may call the sea,

15   Do ebb and flow with tears, the bark thy body is,
Sailing in this salt flood, the winds thy sighs,
Who raging with thy tears and they with them,
Without a sudden calm will overset
Thy tempest-tossed body. How now wife,

20   Have you deliver'd to her our decree?

LADY CAPULET: Ay sir, but she will none, she gives you
thanks,
I would the fool were married to her grave.

CAPULET: Soft take me with you, take me with you wife,

25   How, will she none? Doth she not give us thanks?
Is she not proud? Doth she not count her blest,
Unworthy as she is, that we have wrought
So worthy a gentleman to be her bridegroom?

JULIET: Not proud you have, but thankful that you have:

30   Proud can I never be of what I hate,
But thankful even for hate, that is meant love.

CAPULET: How, how, how how, chop-logic, what is this?

Proud and I thank you, and I thank you not,
And yet not proud mistress minion you?
Thank me no thankings, nor proud me no prouds,
But fettle your fine joints gainst Thursday next,
To go with Paris to Saint Peter's Church: 5
Or I will drag thee on a hurdle thither.
Out you green-sickness carrion, out you baggage,
You tallow-face.   -

LADY CAPULET: Fie, fie, what are you mad?

JULIET: Good father, I beseech you on my knees,   10
Hear me with patience, but to speak a word.
         ⟨She kneels down.⟩

CAPULET: Hang thee young baggage, disobedient wretch,
I tell thee what, get thee to church a' Thursday,
Or never after look me in the face.   15
Speak not, reply not, do not answer me.
My fingers itch, wife: we scarce thought us blest,
That God had lent us but this only child,
But now I see this one is one too much,
And that we have a curse in having her: 20
Out on her hilding.

NURSE: God in heaven bless her:
You are to blame my Lord to rate her so.

CAPULET: And why my Lady wisdom? hold your tongue,
Good prudence, smatter with your gossips, go.   25

NURSE: I speak no treason.

CAPULET: O God ye god-den.

NURSE: May not one speak?

CAPULET: Peace you mumbling fool,
Utter your gravity o'er a gossip's bowl,   30
For here we need it not.

LADY CAPULET: You are too hot.

CAPULET: God's bread, it makes me mad,
   Day, night, hour, tide, time, work, play,
   Alone in company, still my care hath been
   To have her match'd, and having now provided
5   A gentleman of noble parentage,
   Of fair demesnes, youthful, and nobly train'd,
   Stuff'd as they say, with honourable parts,
   Proportion'd as one's thought would wish a man,
   And then to have a wretched puling fool,
10   A whining mammet, in her fortune's tender,
   To answer, I 'll not wed, I cannot love :
   I am too young, I pray you pardon me.
   But and you will not wed, I 'll pardon you.
   Graze where you will, you shall not house with me,
15   Look to 't, think on 't, I do not use to jest.
   Thursday is near, lay hand on heart, advise,
   And you be mine, I 'll give you to my friend,
   And you be not, hang, beg, starve, die in the streets,
   For by my soul I 'll ne'er acknowledge thee,
20   Nor what is mine shall never do thee good :
   Trust to 't, bethink you, I 'll not be forsworn.
                              Exit.
   JULIET: Is there no pity sitting in the clouds
   That sees into the bottom of my grief ?
25   O sweet my Mother cast me not away,
   Delay this marriage for a month, a week,
   Or if you do not, make the bridal bed
   In that dim monument where Tybalt lies.
   LADY CAPULET: Talk not to me, for I 'll not speak a
30   word,
   Do as thou wilt, for I have done with thee.
                              Exit.

JULIET: O God, O Nurse, how shall this be prevented?
My husband is on earth, my faith in heaven,
How shall that faith return again to earth,
Unless that husband send it me from heaven,
By leaving earth? Comfort me, counsel me: 5
Alack, alack, that heaven should practise stratagems
Upon so soft a subject as myself.
What say'st thou, hast thou not a word of joy?
Some comfort Nurse.

NURSE: Faith here it is,   10
Romeo is banish'd and all the world to nothing,
That he dares ne'er come back to challenge you:
Or if he do, it needs must be by stealth.
Then since the case so stands as now it doth,
I think it best you married with the County,   15
O he's a lovely gentleman:
Romeo's a dishclout to him: an eagle Madam
Hath not so green, so quick, so fair an eye
As Paris hath, beshrew my very heart,
I think you are happy in this second match,   20
For it excels your first, or if it did not,
Your first is dead, or 'twere as good he were,
As living here, and you no use of him.

JULIET: Speakest thou from thy heart?

NURSE: And from my soul too,   25
Else beshrew them both.

JULIET: Amen.

NURSE: What?

JULIET: Well thou hast comforted me, marvellous much,
Go in, and tell my Lady I am gone,   30
Having displeas'd my father, to Laurence' cell,
To make confession, and to be absolv'd.

NURSE: Marry I will, and this is wisely done.

Exit.

[*She looks after the Nurse.*]

JULIET: Ancient damnation, O most wicked fiend,
5   Is it more sin to wish me thus forsworn,
       Or to dispraise my Lord with that same tongue,
       Which she hath prais'd him with above compare,
       So many thousand times? Go counsellor,
       Thou and my bosom henceforth shall be twain:
10   I'll to the Friar to know his remedy,
       If all else fail, myself have power to die.

IV.1

Enter Friar and County Paris.

FRIAR LAURENCE: On Thursday sir: the time is very
15   short.
PARIS: My father Capulet will have it so,
       And I am nothing slow to slack his haste.
FRIAR LAURENCE: You say you do not know the Lady's
       mind?
20   Uneven is the course, I like it not.
PARIS: Immoderately she weeps for Tybalt's death,
       And therefore have I little talk'd of love,
       For Venus smiles not in a house of tears.
       Now sir, her father counts it dangerous
25   That she do give her sorrow so much sway:
       And in his wisdom hastes our marriage,
       To stop the inundation of her tears,
       Which too much minded by herself alone
       May be put from her by society.
30   Now do you know the reason of this haste.

FRIAR LAURENCE: I would I knew not why it should be slow'd.

Look sir, here comes the Lady toward my cell.

Enter Juliet.

PARIS: Happily well met, my Lady and my wife. 5

JULIET: That may be sir, when I may be a wife.

PARIS: That may be, must be love, on Thursday next.

JULIET: What must be shall be.

FRIAR LAURENCE: That's a certain text.

PARIS: Come you to make confession to this Father? 10

JULIET: To answer that, I should confess to you.

PARIS: Do not deny to him, that you love me.

JULIET: I will confess to you that I love him.

PARIS: So will ye, I am sure that you love me.

JULIET: If I do so, it will be of more price, 15
Being spoke behind your back, than to your face.

PARIS: Poor soul thy face is much abus'd with tears.

JULIET: The tears have got small victory by that,
For it was bad enough before their spite.

PARIS: Thou wrong'st it more than tears by that report. 20

JULIET: That is no slander sir, which is a truth,
And what I spake, I spake it to my face.

PARIS: Thy face is mine, and thou hast slander'd it.

JULIET: It may be so, for it is not mine own.
Are you at leisure, holy Father now, 25
Or shall I come to you at evening Mass?

FRIAR LAURENCE: My leisure serves me pensive daughter now.
My Lord we must entreat the time alone.

PARIS: God shield, I should disturb devotion, 30
Juliet, on Thursday early will I rouse ye,
Till then adieu, and keep this holy kiss.

Exit.

JULIET: O shut the door, and when thou hast done so,
Come weep with me, past hope, past care, past help.
FRIAR LAURENCE: O Juliet I already know thy grief,
It strains me past the compass of my wits:
5   I hear thou must, and nothing may prorogue it,
On Thursday next be married to this County.
JULIET: Tell me not Friar, that thou hear'st of this,
Unless thou tell me how I may prevent it:
If in thy wisdom thou canst give no help,
10   Do thou but call my resolution wise,
And with this knife I'll help it presently.
God join'd my heart and Romeo's, thou our hands,
And ere this hand by thee to Romeo's seal'd,
Shall be the label to another deed,
15   Or my true heart with treacherous revolt,
Turn to another, this shall slay them both:
Therefore out of thy long experienc'd time,
Give me some present counsel, or behold
'Twixt my extremes and me, this bloody knife
20   Shall play the umpire, arbitrating that,
Which the commission of thy years and art,
Could to no issue of true honour bring:
Be not so long to speak, I long to die,
If what thou speak'st, speak not of remedy.
25 FRIAR LAURENCE: Hold daughter, I do spy a kind of
    hope,
As that is desperate which we would prevent.
If rather than to marry County Paris
Thou hast the strength of will to slay thyself,
30   Then it is likely thou wilt undertake
A thinglike death to chide away this shame,
That cop'st with death himself, to 'scape from it:

And if thou dar'st, I'll give thee remedy.

JULIET: O bid me leap, rather than marry Paris,
From off the battlements of any tower,
Or walk in thievish ways, or bid me lurk
Where serpents are: chain me with roaring bears,   5
Or hide me nightly in a charnel-house,
O'er-cover'd quite with dead men's rattling bones,
With reeky shanks and yellow chapless skulls:
Or bid me go into a new-made grave,
And hide me with a dead man in his shroud,   10
Things that to hear them told, have made me tremble,
And I will do it without fear or doubt,
To live an unstain'd wife to my sweet love.

FRIAR LAURENCE: Hold then, go home, be merry, give
    consent,   15
To marry Paris: Wednesday is to-morrow,
To-morrow night look that thou lie alone,
Let not the Nurse lie with thee in thy chamber:
Take thou this vial, being then in bed,
And this distilled liquor drink thou off,   20
When presently through all thy veins shall run,
A cold and drowsy humour: for no pulse
Shall keep his native progress but surcease,
No warmth, no breath shall testify thou livest,
The roses in thy lips and cheeks shall fade   25
To many ashes, thy eyes' windows fall:
Like death when he shuts up the day of life:
Each part depriv'd of supple government,
Shall stiff and stark, and cold appear like death,
And in this borrow'd likeness of shrunk death   30
Thou shalt continue two and forty hours,
And then awake as from a pleasant sleep.

Now when the Bridegroom in the morning comes,
To rouse thee from thy bed, there art thou dead:
Then as the manner of our country is,
In thy best robes uncovered on the bier,
5 Be borne to burial in thy kindred's grave:
Thou shalt be borne to that same ancient vault,
Where all the kindred of the Capulets lie;
In the mean time against thou shalt awake,
Shall Romeo by my letters know our drift,
10 And hither shall he come, and he and I
Will watch thy waking, and that very night
Shall Romeo bear thee hence to Mantua.
And this shall free thee from this present shame,
If no inconstant toy nor womanish fear,
15 Abate thy valour in the acting it.

JULIET: Give me, give me, O tell not me of fear.

FRIAR LAURENCE: Hold get you gone, be strong and
     prosperous
In this resolve, I'll send a Friar with speed
20 To Mantua, with my letters to thy Lord.

JULIET: Love give me strength, and strength shall help af-
     ford:
Farewell dear Father.

Exeunt.

25   IV. 2

*Enter Capulet, Lady Capulet, Nurse, and Servingmen two
              or three.*

CAPULET: So many guests invite as here are writ,
Sirrah, go hire me twenty cunning cooks.

SERVANT: You shall have none ill sir, for I'll try if they
    can lick their fingers.

CAPULET: How canst thou try them so?

SERVANT: Marry sir, 'tis an ill cook that cannot lick his
    own fingers: therefore he that cannot lick his fingers goes   5
    not with me.

CAPULET: Go be gone,

               Exit.

    We shall be much unfurnish'd for this time:

    What is my daughter gone to Friar Laurence?   10

NURSE: Ay forsooth.

CAPULET: Well, he may chance to do some good on her,
    A peevish self-will'd harlotry it is.

             Enter Juliet.

NURSE: See where she comes from shrift with merry 15
    look.

CAPULET: How now my headstrong, where have you
    been gadding?

JULIET: Where I have learn'd me to repent the sin
    Of disobedient opposition,   20
    To you and your behests, and am enjoin'd
    By holy Laurence to fall prostrate here,
    To beg your pardon, pardon I beseech you,
    Henceforward I am ever rul'd by you.

CAPULET: Send for the County, go tell him of this, 25
    I'll have this knot knit up to-morrow morning.

JULIET: I met the youthful Lord at Laurence' cell,
    And gave him what becomed love I might,
    Not stepping o'er the bounds of modesty.

CAPULET: Why I am glad on't, this is well, stand up, 30
    This is as't should be, let me see the County:
    Ay marry go I say and fetch him hither.

Now afore God, this reverend holy Friar,
All our whole city is much bound to him.
JULIET: Nurse, will you go with me into my closet,
To help me sort such needful ornaments,
5 As you think fit to furnish me tomorrow?
LADY CAPULET: No not till Thursday, there is time
  enough.
CAPULET: Go Nurse, go with her, we'll to church to-mor-
  row.
10   *Exeunt Juliet and Nurse.*
LADY CAPULET: We shall be short in our provision,
'Tis now near night.
CAPULET: Tush, I will stir about,
And all things shall be well, I warrant thee wife:
15 Go thou to Juliet, help to deck up her,
I'll not to bed to-night, let me alone:
I'll play the housewife for this once, what ho?
They are all forth, well I will walk myself
To County Paris, to prepare up him
20 Against to-morrow, my heart is wondrous light,
Since this same wayward girl is so reclaim'd.
        Exeunt.

IV. 3

Enter Juliet and Nurse.
25 JULIET: Ay those attires are best, but gentle Nurse
I pray thee leave me to myself to-night:
For I have need of many orisons,
To move the heavens to smile upon my state,
Which well thou know'st, is cross and full of sin.
30   *Enter Lady Capulet.*

LADY CAPULET: What are you busy ho? Need you my
   help?

JULIET: No Madam, we have cull'd such necessaries
   As are behoveful for our state to-morrow:
   So please you, let me now be left alone,   5
   And let the Nurse this night sit up with you,
   For I am sure you have your hands full all,
   In this so sudden business.

LADY CAPULET: Good night.
   Get thee to bed and rest, for thou hast need   10
         Exeunt Lady Capulet and Nurse.

JULIET: Farewell, God knows when we shall meet again.
   I have a faint cold fear thrills through my veins,
   That almost freezes up the heat of life:
   I'll call them back again to comfort me.   15
   Nurse, what should she do here?
   My dismal scene I needs must act alone.
   Come vial, what if this mixture do not work at all?
   Shall I be married then to-morrow morning?
   No, no, this shall forbid it, lie thou there.   20
   What if it be a poison which the Friar
   Subtly hath minister'd to have me dead,
   Lest in this marriage he should be dishonour'd,
   Because he married me before to Romeo?
   I fear it is, and yet methinks it should not,   25
   For he hath still been tried a holy man.
   How if when I am laid into the tomb,
   I wake before the time that Romeo
   Come to redeem me, there's a fearful point:
   Shall I not then be stifled in the vault?   30
   To whose foul mouth no healthsome air breathes in,
   And there die strangled ere my Romeo comes.

Or if I live, is it not very like,
The horrible conceit of death and night,
Together with the terror of the place,
As in a vault, an ancient receptacle,
5   Where for this many hundred years the bones
Of all my buried ancestors are pack'd,
Where bloody Tybalt yet but green in earth,
Lies festering in his shroud, where as they say,
At some hours in the night, spirits resort:
10 Alack, alack, is it not like that I
So early waking, what with loathsome smells,
And shrieks like mandrakes torn out of the earth,
That living mortals hearing them run mad:
Or if I walk, shall I not be distraught,
15 Environed with all these hideous fears,
And madly play with my forefathers' joints?
And pluck the mangled Tybalt from his shroud,
And in this rage with some great kinsman's bone,
As with a club dash out my desperate brains.
20 O look, methinks I see my cousin's ghost,
Seeking out Romeo that did spit his body
Upon a rapier's point: stay Tybalt, stay!
Romeo, Romeo, Romeo, here's drink, I drink to thee.
⟨*She falls upon her bed within the curtains.*⟩

IV.4

Enter Lady Capulet and Nurse ⟨*with herbs*⟩.

LADY CAPULET: Hold take these keys and fetch more
spices Nurse.

NURSE: They call for dates and quinces in the Pastry.

30   *Enter Capulet.*

CAPULET: Come, stir, stir, stir, the second cock hath
    crow'd,
  The curfew-bell hath rung, 'tis three o'clock:
  Look to the bak'd meats, good Angelica,
  Spare not for cost.   5

NURSE: Go you cot-quean go,
  Get you to bed, faith you'll be sick to-morrow
  For this night's watching.

CAPULET: No not a whit, what I have watch'd ere now,
  All night for lesser cause, and ne'er been sick.   10

LADY CAPULET: Ay you have been a mouse-hunt in your
    time,
  But I will watch you from such watching now.
            Exeunt Lady Capulet and Nurse.

CAPULET: A jealous-hood, a jealous-hood,   15
    Enter three or four with spits, and logs, and baskets.
  Now fellow, what is there?

FELLOW: Things for the cook sir, but I know not what.

CAPULET: Make haste, make haste, sirrah, fetch drier logs.
  Call Peter, he will show thee where they are.   20

FELLOW: I have a head sir, that will find out logs,
  And never trouble Peter for the matter.
            Exeunt.

CAPULET: Mass and well said, a merry whoreson, ha,
  Thou shalt be logger-head; good father, 'tis day.   25
            Play music.
  The County will be here with music straight,
  For so he said he would, I hear him near.
  Nurse, wife, what ho, what Nurse I say!
            Enter Nurse.   30
  Go waken Juliet, go and trim her up,
  I'll go and chat with Paris, hie, make haste,

Make haste, the bridegroom, he is come already,
Make haste I say.

Exit.

IV. 5

5 NURSE: Mistress what mistress, Juliet, fast I warrant her
  she,
  Why lamb, why Lady, fie you slug-a-bed,
  Why love I say, Madam, sweet-heart, why Bride:
  What not a word, you take your pennyworths now,
10 Sleep for a week, for the next night I warrant
  The County Paris hath set up his rest,
  That you shall rest but little, God forgive me;
  Marry and amen: how sound is she asleep:
  I needs must wake her: Madam, Madam, Madam,
15 Ay, let the County take you in your bed,
  He'll fright you up i' faith, will it not be?
  What dress'd, and in your clothes, and down again?
  I must needs wake you, Lady, Lady, Lady.
  Alas, alas, help, help, my Lady's dead.
20 O well-a-day that ever I was born,
  Some aqua-vitae ho, my Lord, my Lady.

Enter Lady Capulet.

LADY CAPULET: What noise is here?
NURSE: O lamentable day.
25 LADY CAPULET: What is the matter?
NURSE: Look, look, O heavy day!
LADY CAPULET: O me, O me, my child, my only life.
  Revive, look up, or I will die with thee:
  Help, help, call help.
30   *Enter Capulet.*

CAPULET: For shame bring Juliet forth, her Lord is come.

NURSE: She's dead: deceas'd, she's dead, alack the day.

LADY CAPULET: Alack the day, she's dead, she's dead, she's dead.

CAPULET: Ha let me see her, out alas she's cold,   5
Her blood is settled and her joints are stiff:
Life and these lips have long been separated:
Death lies on her like an untimely frost,
Upon the sweetest flower of all the field.

NURSE: O lamentable day!   10

LADY CAPULET: O woeful time!

CAPULET: Death that hath ta'en her hence to make me wail,
Ties up my tongue and will not let me speak.
                    Enter Friar and the County.   15

FRIAR LAURENCE: Come, is the Bride ready to go to church?

CAPULET: Ready to go but never to return.
O son, the night before thy wedding day
Hath death lain with thy wife: there she lies,   20
Flower as she was, deflower'd by him,
Death is my son-in-law, death is my heir,
My daughter he hath wedded. I will die,
And leave him all life living, all is Death's.

PARIS: Have I thought long to see this morning's face,   25
And doth it give me such a sight as this?

LADY CAPULET: Accurst, unhappy, wretched hateful day,
Most miserable hour that e'er time saw,
In lasting labour of his pilgrimage.
But one poor one, one poor and loving child,   30
But one thing to rejoice and solace in,
And cruel death hath catch'd it from my sight.

NURSE: O woe, O woeful, woeful, woeful day,
Most lamentable day, most woeful day
That ever, ever, I did yet behold.
O day, O day, O day, O hateful day,
5   Never was seen so black a day as this,
O woeful day, O woeful day.
PARIS: Beguil'd, divorced, wronged, spited, slain,
Most detestable death, by thee beguil'd,
By cruel, cruel thee, quite overthrown:
10   O love, O life, not life, but love in death.
CAPULET: Despis'd, distressed, hated, martyr'd, kill'd,
Uncomfortable time, why cam'st thou now
To murther, murther our solemnity?
O child, O child, my soul and not my child,
15   Dead art thou, alack my child is dead,
And with my child my joys are buried.
FRIAR LAURENCE: Peace ho for shame, confusion's care
lives not,
In these confusions: heaven and yourself
20   Had part in this fair maid, now heaven hath all,
And all the better is it for the maid:
Your part in her, you could not keep from death,
But heaven keeps his part in eternal life:
The most you sought was her promotion,
25   For 'twas your heaven she should be advanc'd,
And weep ye now, seeing she is advanc'd
Above the clouds, as high as heaven itself.
O in this love, you love your child so ill,
That you run mad, seeing that she is well:
30   She's not well married, that lives married long,
But she's best married, that dies married young.
Dry up your tears, and stick your rosemary

On this fair corse, and as the custom is,
And in her best array bear her to church:
For though fond nature bids us all lament,
Yet nature's tears are reason's merriment.

CAPULET: All things that we ordained festival,   5
Turn from their office to black funeral:
Our instruments to melancholy bells,
Our wedding cheer to a sad burial feast:
Our solemn hymns to sullen dirges change:
Our bridal flowers serve for a buried corse: 10
And all things change them to the contrary.

FRIAR LAURENCE: Sir go you in, and Madam go with
      him,
And go Sir Paris, every one prepare
To follow this fair corse unto her grave: 15
The heavens do lour upon you for some ill:
Move them no more, by crossing their high will.
⟨*They all but the Nurse go forth, casting rosemary on her
      and shutting the curtains.*⟩
                Enter Musicians.   20

MUSICIAN: Faith we may put up our pipes and be gone.

NURSE: Honest good fellows, ah put up, put up,
For well you know, this is a pitiful case.
                Exit.

FIDDLER: Ay by my troth, the case may be amended.   25
                Enter Peter.

PETER: Musicians, O musicians, *Heart's ease, Heart's ease,*
      O, and you will have me live, play *Heart's ease.*

MUSICIAN: Why *Heart's ease?*

PETER: O musicians, because my heart itself plays, My   30
      heart is full: O play me some merry dump to comfort
      me.

MUSICIAN: Not a dump we, 'tis no time to play now.

PETER: You will not then?

MUSICIAN: No.

PETER: I will then give it you soundly.

5 MUSICIAN: What will you give us?

PETER: No money on my faith, but the gleek. I will give you the minstrel.

MUSICIAN: Then will I give you the serving-creature.

PETER: Then will I lay the serving-creature's dagger on
10   your pate. I will carry no crotchets, I'll re you, I'll fa you, do you note me?

MUSICIAN: And you re us, and fa us, you note us.

1 MUSICIAN: Pray you put up your dagger, and put out your wit.

15   Then have at you with my wit.

PETER: I will dry-beat you with an iron wit, and put up my iron dagger.

Answer me like men.

When griping griefs the heart doth wound, then music
20   with her silver sound,

Why silver sound, why music with her silver sound?

What say you, Simon Catling?

MUSICIAN: Marry sir, because silver hath a sweet sound.

PETER: Prates, what say you Hugh Rebick?

25 2 MUSICIAN: I say silver sound, because musicians sound for silver.

PETER: Prates too, what say you James Soundpost?

3 MUSICIAN: Faith I know not what to say.

PETER: O I cry you mercy, you are the singer. I will say
30   for you, it is music with her silver sound, because musicians have no gold for sounding:

Then music with her silver sound

With speedy help doth lend redress.

MUSICIAN: What a pestilent knave is this same?

2 MUSICIAN: Hang him Jack, come we'll in here, tarry
    for the mourners, and stay dinner.

Exeunt.

    5

V.1

Enter Romeo.

ROMEO: If I may trust the flattering truth of sleep,
    My dreams presage some joyful news at hand,
    My bosom's Lord sits lightly in his throne: 10
    And all this day an unaccustom'd spirit,
    Lifts me above the ground with cheerful thoughts.
    I dreamt my Lady came and found me dead,
    (Strange dream that gives a dead man leave to think:)
    And breath'd such life with kisses in my lips,   15
    That I reviv'd and was an Emperor.
    Ah me, how sweet is love itself possess'd
    When but love's shadows are so rich in joy.

Enter Romeo's man Balthasar, ⟨booted⟩.

    News from Verona, how now Balthasar,   20
    Dost thou not bring me letters from the Friar?
    How doth my Lady? Is my father well?
    How doth my Lady Juliet? That I ask again,
    For nothing can be ill, if she be well.

MAN: Then she is well, and nothing can be ill,   25
    Her body sleeps in Capels' monument,
    And her immortal part with angels lives.
    I saw her laid low in her kindred's vault,
    And presently took post to tell it you:
    O pardon me for bringing these ill news,   30

Since you did leave it for my office sir.

ROMEO: Is it e'en so? Then I deny you stars.
Thou know'st my lodging, get me ink and paper,
And hire post-horses, I will hence to-night.

5 MAN: I do beseech you sir, have patience:
Your looks are pale and wild, and do import
Some misadventure.

ROMEO: Tush, thou art deceiv'd,
Leave me, and do the thing I bid thee do.

10 Hast thou no letters to me from the Friar?

MAN: No my good Lord.

Exit.

ROMEO: No matter: get thee gone,
And hire those horses, I'll be with thee straight.

15 Well Juliet, I will lie with thee to-night:
Let's see for means: O mischief thou art swift,
To enter in the thoughts of desperate men.
I do remember an apothecary,
And hereabouts a' dwells, which late I noted

20 In tatter'd weeds with overwhelming brows,
Culling of simples, meagre were his looks,
Sharp misery had worn him to the bones:
And in his needy shop a tortoise hung,
An alligator stuff'd, and other skins

25 Of ill-shaped fishes, and about his shelves
A beggarly account of empty boxes,
Green earthen pots, bladders and musty seeds,
Remnants of packthread, and old cakes of roses
Were thinly scatter'd, to make up a show.

30 Noting this penury, to myself I said,
An if a man did need a poison now,
Whose sale is present death in Mantua,

Here lives a caitiff wretch would sell it him.
O this same thought did but forerun my need,
And this same needy man must sell it me.
As I remember this should be the house,
Being holy day the beggar's shop is shut.   5
What ho! Apothecary!

Enter Apothecary.

APOTHECARY: Who calls so loud?
ROMEO: Come hither man, I see that thou art poor,
  Hold, there is forty ducats, let me have   10
  A dram of poison, such soon-speeding gear,
  As will disperse itself through all the veins,
  That the life-weary-taker may fall dead,
  And that the trunk may be discharg'd of breath,
  As violently, as hasty powder fir'd   15
  Doth hurry from the fatal cannon's womb.
APOTHECARY: Such mortal drugs I have, but Mantua's
  law
  Is death to any he that utters them.
ROMEO: Art thou so bare and full of wretchedness,   20
  And fear'st to die? Famine is in thy cheeks,
  Need and oppression starveth in thy eyes,
  Contempt and beggary hangs upon thy back:
  The world is not thy friend, nor the world's law,
  The world affords no law to make thee rich: 25
  Then be not poor, but break it and take this.
APOTHECARY: My poverty, but not my will consents.
ROMEO: I pay thy poverty and not thy will.
APOTHECARY: Put this in any liquid thing you will
  And drink it off, and if you had the strength   30
  Of twenty men, it would dispatch you straight.
ROMEO: There is thy gold, worse poison to men's souls,

Doing more murther in this loathsome world,
Than these poor compounds that thou mayst not sell.
I sell thee poison, thou hast sold me none,
Farewell, buy food, and get thyself in flesh.
5   Come cordial and not poison, go with me
To Juliet's grave, for there must I use thee.
Exeunt.

V. 2

Enter Friar John to Friar Laurence.

10   FRIAR JOHN: Holy Franciscan Friar, brother, ho.
Enter Laurence.

FRIAR LAURENCE: This same should be the voice of Friar
John.
Welcome from Mantua, what says Romeo?
15   Or if his mind be writ, give me his letter.

FRIAR JOHN: Going to find a bare-foot brother out,
One of our order to associate me,
Here in this city visiting the sick,
And finding him, the searchers of the town
20   Suspecting that we both were in a house
Where the infectious pestilence did reign,
Seal'd up the doors, and would not let us forth,
So that my speed to Mantua there was stay'd.

FRIAR LAURENCE: Who bare my letter then to Romeo?

25   FRIAR JOHN: I could not send it, here it is again,
Nor get a messenger to bring it thee,
So fearful were they of infection.

FRIAR LAURENCE: Unhappy fortune, by my Brother-
hood,
30   The letter was not nice but full of charge,

Of dear import, and the neglecting it,
May do much danger: Friar John go hence,
Get me an iron crow, and bring it straight
Unto my cell.

FRIAR JOHN: Brother I'll go and bring it thee.   5
Exit.

FRIAR LAURENCE: Now must I to the monument alone,
Within this three hours will fair Juliet wake,
She will beshrew me much that Romeo
Hath had no notice of these accidents: 10
But I will write again to Mantua,
And keep her at my cell till Romeo come,
Poor living corse, clos'd in a dead man's tomb.
Exit.

V. 3   15

*Enter County Paris and his Page, ⟨with flowers, and
sweet water.⟩*

PARIS: Give me thy torch boy, hence and stand aloof,
Yet put it out, for I would not be seen:
Under yond yew-trees lay thee all along,   20
Holding thine ear close to the hollow ground,
So shall no foot upon the churchyard tread,
Being loose, unfirm with digging up of graves,
But thou shalt hear it: whistle then to me,
As signal that thou hear'st some thing approach.   25
Give me those flowers. Do as I bid thee, go.

PAGE: I am almost afraid to stand alone
Here in the churchyard, yet I will adventure.
⟨*Paris strews the tomb with flowers.*⟩

PARIS: Sweet flower, with flowers thy bridal bed I strew:
    O woe, thy canopy is dust and stones,
    Which with sweet water nightly I will dew,
    Or wanting that, with tears distill'd by moans,
5   The obsequies that I for thee will keep,
    Nightly shall be to strew thy grave and weep.
The Page whistles and calls: My Lord.
    The boy gives warning, something doth approach,
    What cursed foot wanders this way to-night,
10   To cross my obsequies, and true love's rite?
    What with a torch? Muffle me night a while.
Enter Romeo and Balthasar ⟨with a torch, mattock, and a
    crow of iron⟩.

ROMEO: Give me that mattock and the wrenching iron,
15   Hold take this letter, early in the morning
    See thou deliver it to my Lord and father,
    Give me the light; upon thy life I charge thee
    Whate'er thou hear'st or seest, stand all aloof,
    And do not interrupt me in my course.
20   Why I descend into this bed of death,
    Is partly to behold my Lady's face:
    But chiefly to take thence from her dead finger,
    A precious ring: a ring that I must use,
    In dear employment, therefore hence be gone:
25   But if thou jealous dost return to pry
    In what I farther shall intend to do,
    By heaven I will tear thee joint by joint,
    And strew this hungry churchyard with thy limbs:
    The time and my intents are savage wild,
30   More fierce and more inexorable far,
    Than empty tigers, or the roaring sea.
MAN: I will be gone sir, and not trouble ye.

ROMEO: So shalt thou show me friendship, take thou that,
  Live and be prosperous, and farewell good fellow.
MAN: For all this same, I'll hide me hereabout,
  His looks I fear, and his intents I doubt.
         ⟨*Romeo opens the tomb.*⟩   5
ROMEO: Thou detestable maw, thou womb of death,
  Gorg'd with the dearest morsel of the earth:
  Thus I enforce thy rotten jaws to open,
  And in despite I'll cram thee with more food.
PARIS: This is that banish'd haughty Montague,   10
  That murder'd my love's cousin, with which grief
  It is suppos'd the fair creature died,
  And here is come to do some villainous shame
  To the dead bodies: I will apprehend him.
  Stop thy unhallow'd toil, vile Montague: 15
  Can vengeance be pursued further than death?
  Condemned villain, I do apprehend thee,
  Obey and go with me, for thou must die.
ROMEO: I must indeed, and therefore came I hither:
  Good gentle youth tempt not a desperate man,   20
  Fly hence and leave me, think upon these gone,
  Let them affright thee. I beseech thee youth,
  Put not another sin upon my head,
  By urging me to fury. O be gone,
  By heaven I love thee better than myself,   25
  For I come hither arm'd against myself:
  Stay not, be gone, live, and hereafter say,
  A madman's mercy bid thee run away.
PARIS: I do defy thy conjurations,
  And apprehend thee for a felon here.   30
ROMEO: Wilt thou provoke me? Then have at thee boy.
         ⟨*They fight.*⟩

PAGE: O Lord they fight, I will go call the watch.

Exit.

PARIS: O I am slain, if thou be merciful,
Open the tomb, lay me with Juliet.

5   *Dies.*

ROMEO: In faith I will, let me peruse this face:
Mercutio's kinsman, noble County Paris,
What said my man, when my betossed soul
Did not attend him as we rode? I think

10   He told me Paris should have married Juliet.
Said he not so? Or did I dream it so?
Or am I mad, hearing him talk of Juliet,
To think it was so? O give me thy hand,
One writ with me in sour misfortune's book,

15   I'll bury thee in a triumphant grave.
A grave, O no, a lantern, slaughter'd youth:
For here lies Juliet, and her beauty makes
This vault a feasting presence full of light.
Death lie thou there by a dead man interr'd.

20   How oft when men are at the point of death,
Have they been merry! which their keepers call
A lightning before death: O how may I
Call this a lightning! O my Love, my wife,
Death that hath suck'd the honey of thy breath,

25   Hath had no power yet upon thy beauty:
Thou art not conquer'd, beauty's ensign yet
Is crimson in thy lips and in thy cheeks,
And death's pale flag is not advanced there.
Tybalt liest thou there in thy bloody sheet?

30   O what more favour can I do to thee,
Than with that hand that cut thy youth in twain,
To sunder his that was thine enemy?

Forgive me cousin. Ah dear Juliet
Why art thou yet so fair? Shall I believe
That unsubstantial death is amorous,
And that the lean abhorred monster keeps
Thee here in dark to be his paramour? 5
For fear of that I still will stay with thee,
And never from this palace of dim night
Depart again: here, here will I remain,
With worms that are thy chamber-maids: O here
Will I set up my everlasting rest: 10
And shake the yoke of inauspicious stars,
From this world-wearied flesh: eyes look your last:
Arms take your last embrace: and lips, O you
The doors of breath, seal with a righteous kiss
A dateless bargain to engrossing death: 15
Come bitter conduct, come unsavoury guide,
Thou desperate pilot, now at once run on
The dashing rocks, thy sea-sick weary bark:
Here's to my love. O true apothecary:
Thy drugs are quick. Thus with a kiss I die. ⟨*Falls.*⟩ 20
  Enter Friar with a lantern, crow, and spade.
FRIAR LAURENCE: Saint Francis be my speed, how oft to-
  night
Have my old feet stumbled at graves? Who's there?
MAN: Here's one, a friend, and one that knows you well. 25
FRIAR LAURENCE: Bliss be upon you. Tell me good my
  friend
What torch is yond that vainly lends his light
To grubs and eyeless skulls: as I discern,
It burneth in the Capels' monument. 30
MAN: It doth so holy sir, and there's my master,
  One that you love.

FRIAR LAURENCE: Who is it?

MAN: Romeo.

FRIAR LAURENCE: How long hath he been there?

MAN: Full half an hour.

5   FRIAR LAURENCE: Go with me to the vault.

MAN: I dare not sir.

My master knows not but I am gone hence,
And fearfully did menace me with death,
If I did stay to look on his intents.

10   FRIAR LAURENCE: Stay, then I'll go alone, fear comes
        upon me.

O much I fear some ill unthrifty thing.
        ⟨*Friar stoops and looks on the blood and weapons.*⟩

MAN: As I did sleep under this yew-tree here,

15   I dreamt my master and another fought,
        And that my master slew him.

FRIAR LAURENCE: Romeo.

Alack, alack, what blood is this which stains
The stony entrance of this sepulchre?

20   What mean these masterless and gory swords
        To lie discolour'd by this place of peace?
        Romeo, oh pale! who else, what Paris too?
        And steep'd in blood? Ah what an unkind hour
        Is guilty of this lamentable chance!

25   The Lady stirs.
                ⟨*Juliet rises.*⟩

JULIET: O comfortable Friar, where is my Lord?
        I do remember well where I should be:
        And there I am, where is my Romeo?

30   FRIAR LAURENCE: I hear some noise Lady, come from
        that nest
        Of death, contagion and unnatural sleep:

A greater power than we can contradict
Hath thwarted our intents, come, come away,
Thy husband in thy bosom there lies dead:
And Paris too: come, I'll dispose of thee,
Among a Sisterhood of holy Nuns: 5
Stay not to question, for the watch is coming,
Come go good Juliet, I dare no longer stay.
                        Exit Friar Laurence.
JULIET: Go get thee hence, for I will not away.
   What's here? A cup clos'd in my true love's hand?   10
   Poison I see hath been his timeless end:
   O churl, drunk all? And left no friendly drop
   To help me after, I will kiss thy lips,
   Haply some poison yet doth hang on them,
   To make me die with a restorative.   15
   Thy lips are warm.
                        Enter Boy and Watch.
WATCH: Lead boy, which way.
JULIET: Yea noise? Then I'll be brief. O happy dagger.
   This is thy sheath, there rust and let me die.   20
                ⟨*She stabs herself and falls.*⟩
PAGE: This is the place, there where the torch doth burn.
WATCH: The ground is bloody, search about the church-
      yard.
   Go some of you, who'er you find attach.   25
   Pitiful sight, here lies the County slain,
   And Juliet bleeding, warm, and newly dead:
   Who here hath lain this two days buried.
   Go tell the Prince, run to the Capulets,
   Raise up the Montagues, some others search,   30
   We see the ground whereon these woes do lie,
   But the true ground of all these piteous woes

We cannot without circumstance descry.

Enter Romeo's man.

2 WATCH: Here's Romeo's man, we found him in the churchyard.

5 1 WATCH: Hold him in safety till the Prince come hither.

Enter Friar and another Watchman.

3 WATCH: Here is a Friar that trembles, sighs, and weeps,
We took this mattock and this spade from him,
As he was coming from this churchyard's side.

10 1 WATCH: A great suspicion, stay the Friar too.

Enter the Prince.

PRINCE: What misadventure is so early up,
That calls our person from our morning rest?

Enter Capulet and his Wife.

15 CAPULET: What should it be that they so shriek abroad?

LADY CAPULET: The people in the street cry Romeo,
Some Juliet, and some Paris, and all run
With open outcry toward our monument.

PRINCE: What fear is this which startles in your ears?

20 1 WATCH: Sovereign, here lies the County Paris slain,
And Romeo dead, and Juliet dead before,
Warm and new-kill'd.

PRINCE: Search, seek and know how this foul murder comes.

25 1 WATCH: Here is a Friar, and slaughter'd Romeo's man,
With instruments upon them, fit to open
These dead men's tombs.

CAPULET: O heavens! O wife look how our daughter bleeds!

30 This dagger hath mista'en, for lo his house
Is empty on the back of Montague,
And it mis-sheath'd in my daughter's bosom.

LADY CAPULET: O me, this sight of death, is as a bell
  That warns my old age to a sepulchre.
              Enter Montague.

PRINCE: Come Montague, for thou art early up
  To see thy son and heir, now early down.   5

MONTAGUE: Alas my liege, my wife is dead to-night,
  Grief of my son's exile hath stopp'd her breath.
  What further woe conspires against mine age?

PRINCE: Look and thou shalt see.

MONTAGUE: O thou untaught, what manners is in this,   10
  To press before thy father to a grave?

PRINCE: Seal up the mouth of outrage for a while,
  Till we can clear these ambiguities,
  And know their spring, their head, their true descent,
  And then will I be general of your woes,   15
  And lead you even to death: meantime forbear,
  And let mischance be slave to patience:
  Bring forth the parties of suspicion.

FRIAR LAURENCE: I am the greatest able to do least,
  Yet most suspected as the time and place   20
  Doth make against me of this direful murther:
  And here I stand both to impeach and purge
  Myself condemned, and myself excus'd.

PRINCE: Then say at once what thou dost know in this.

FRIAR LAURENCE: I will be brief, for my short date of   25
    breath
  Is not so long as is a tedious tale.
  Romeo there dead, was husband to that Juliet,
  And she there dead, that Romeo's faithful wife:
  I married them, and their stol'n marriage-day   30
  Was Tybalt's dooms-day, whose untimely death
  Banish'd the new-made bridegroom from this city:

For whom, and not for Tybalt, Juliet pin'd.
You to remove that siege of grief from her
Betroth'd and would have married her perforce
To County Paris. Then comes she to me,
And with wild looks bid me devise some mean   5
To rid her from this second marriage,
Or in my cell there would she kill herself.
Then gave I her (so tutor'd by my art)
A sleeping potion, which so took effect
As I intended, for it wrought on her   10
The form of death. Meantime I writ to Romeo
That he should hither come, as this dire night,
To help to take her from her borrow'd grave,
Being the time the potion's force should cease.
But he which bore my letter, Friar John,   15
Was stay'd by accident, and yesternight
Return'd my letter back. Then all alone,
At the prefixed hour of her waking
Came I to take her from her kindred's vault,
Meaning to keep her closely at my cell,   20
Till I conveniently could send to Romeo.
But when I came, some minute ere the time
Of her awaking, here untimely lay,
The noble Paris, and true Romeo dead.
She wakes, and I entreated her come forth   25
And bear this work of heaven with patience:
But then a noise did scare me from the tomb,
And she too desperate would not go with me:
But as it seems, did violence on herself.
All this I know, and to the marriage   30
Her Nurse is privy: and if aught in this
Miscarried by my fault, let my old life

Be sacrific'd some hour before his time,
Unto the rigour of severest law.
PRINCE: We still have known thee for a holy man.
  Where's Romeo's man? What can he say to this?
MAN: I brought my master news of Juliet's death,   5
  And then in post he came from Mantua,
  To this same place, to this same monument.
  This letter he early bid me give his father,
  And threaten'd me with death, going in the vault,
  If I departed not, and left him there.   10
PRINCE: Give me the letter, I will look on it.
  Where is the County's page that rais'd the Watch?
  Sirrah, what made your master in this place?
PAGE: He came with flowers to strew his Lady's grave,
  And bid me stand aloof, and so I did: 15
  Anon comes one with light to ope the tomb,
  And by and by my master drew on him,
  And then I ran away to call the Watch.
PRINCE: This letter doth make good the Friar's words,
  Their course of love, the tidings of her death: 20
  And here he writes, that he did buy a poison
  Of a poor 'pothecary, and therewithal,
  Came to this vault, to die and lie with Juliet.
  Where be these enemies? Capulet, Montague?
  See what a scourge is laid upon your hate!   25
  That heaven finds means to kill your joys with love,
  And I for winking at your discords too,
  Have lost a brace of kinsmen: all are punish'd.
CAPULET: O brother Montague, give me thy hand,
  This is my daughter's jointure, for no more   30
  Can I demand.
MONTAGUE: But I can give thee more,

For I will raise her statue in pure gold,
That whiles Verona by that name is known,
There shall no figure at such rate be set,
As that of true and faithful Juliet.

5 CAPULET: As rich shall Romeo's by his Lady's lie,
Poor sacrifices of our enmity.

PRINCE: A glooming peace this morning with it brings,
The Sun for sorrow will not show his head:
Go hence to have more talk of these sad things,

10 Some shall be pardon'd, and some punished.
For never was a story of more woe,
Than this of Juliet and her Romeo.

Exeunt.

NOTES

References are to the page and line of this edition; there are 32 lines to the full page.

Chorus: Shakespeare seldom uses a Chorus (or Presenter) to introduce and explain the action, though it is common in the plays of other dramatists. P. 31 L. 2

star-cross'd: thwarted by Fate. P. 31 L. 8

two hours' traffic: Two hours was the regular time for an Elizabethan play. Since the theatre was small, the actors could speak rapidly, and there was no scenery to be shifted. P. 31 L. 14

carry coals: do dirty work. P. 32 L. 4

colliers . . . choler . . . collar: Puns on these three words all sounding alike are common. *In choler:* in anger. P. 32 LL. 5-8

take the wall: i.e. the best part of the road where the ground was higher and drier. P. 32 L. 15

bite my thumb: an insulting gesture made by snicking the thumb-nail on the upper teeth. P. 33 L. 15

heartless hinds: a fourfold pun on hinds (= both *deer* and *servants*) without their *harts* and *feelings.* P. 34 LL. 9-10

partisans: spear with a long heavy head, used for street or passage fighting. P. 34 L. 18

long sword: the ancient English weapon, which in the 1590's was giving place to the new fashioned light rapier. See Note on p. 69, l. 27. P. 34 L. 22

neighbour-stained: stained with neighbour's blood. P. 35 L. 1

mistemper'd: tempered for an evil purpose. P. 35 L. 6

Cast . . . ornaments: discard the ornaments of peaceful life. P. 35 L. 12

abroach: open – literally of a cask. P. 35 L. 26

with beauty dies her store: i.e. her beauty dies with her P. 39 L. 17

unless she has children. This lament – that unless a beautiful being marries and leaves children it will perish utterly – is the theme of the first seventeen of Shakespeare's sonnets.

P. 40 L. 1   *happy masks:* When Elizabethan ladies appeared in public in the open air they commonly wore masks, usually black, but sometimes coloured.

P. 40 LL. 6–7 *What doth her beauty . . . passing fair:* i.e. her beauty will only serve to show how much more beautiful is my own Lady.

P. 40 L. 9   *pay that doctrine:* pay for that teaching.

P. 40 L. 13   *bound:* bound over to keep the peace.

P. 40 L. 27   *Lady of my earth:* 'she is all the world to me'; or else *earth:* body (as later, p. 57, l. 8).

P. 41 L. 9   *Such comfort . . . :* i.e. when young men feel the spring in their veins.

P. 41 LL. 23–4 *shoemaker . . . yard:* He mixes his metaphors, as is usual with Shakespeare's clowns.

P. 41 L. 28   *in good time:* i.e. what good luck, for he sees the gentlemen approaching who will be able to read his message.

P. 42 LL. 9–11 *bound . . . tormented:* This was the usual treatment of a madman.

P. 42 L. 12   *God-den:* God give you good even.

P. 44 L. 2   *lady-bird:* used as a term of affection, but it also had a bad meaning – 'tart'. The Nurse realizes that she has used the wrong word.

P. 44 L. 16   *Lammas-tide:* 1 August.

P. 44 LL. 23–4 *'Tis since the Earthquake now eleven years:* Earthquakes are so rare in England that some critics have assumed that Shakespeare was referring to an earthquake which occurred on 6 April 1580, and have accordingly dated the play 1591. But 'twere to consider too curiously to consider so, for the Nurse is notoriously muddled in her dates, and no one in the audience

would have remembered the exact year of an event
so long past.

wormwood: because bitter, and so distasteful.   P. 44 LL. 25–6

I do bear a brain: 'what a head I've got.'   P. 44 LL. 27–8

Shake . . . dove-house: not satisfactorily explained.   P. 44 LL. 30–1

high-lone: all by its little self.   P. 45 L. 1

holidame: for halidom, sacred rite on which an oath   P. 45 L. 7
could be taken.

said ay . . . say I: Puns on 'ay' and 'I' are common   P. 45 LL. 20–1
in Elizabethan literature, and more marked since both
words were often spelt 'I'.

man of wax: the very model of what a man should be.   P. 46 L. 7

Read o'er the volume: Lady Capulet's speech is full of   P. 46 L. 13
the elaborate metaphors and conceits of which Shakespeare in his early work was over-fond. She plays
upon the various images to be found in the notion of
a book.

obscur'd . . . margent: At this time explanatory notes   P. 46 LL. 17–18
in learned and obscure books were usually printed in
the margin.

Maskers: The entertainment at Capulet's house is a   P. 47 L. 10
masque, at which the guests wore masks, often of fan-
tastic design.

this speech: Elizabethan entertainments were elabor-   P. 47 L. 11
ate. When uninvited maskers wished to attend it was
customary to announce their coming by sending a-
head a messenger, symbolically garbed, to make a
suitable speech. Benvolio replies that it is out of
date to have such elaborate formality (*prolixity*) as to
have one of the party dressed up like Cupid, or the
like.

Nor no . . . entrance: These two lines are found only   P. 47 LL. 17–18
in the First Quarto.

measure: formal stately dance in which the dancers   P. 47 L. 20
paced round the floor.

P. 48 l. 13 *cote:* pass by. The Folio reads 'quote'. Mercutio means that he does not care whether his face is as ugly as a mask.

P. 48 l. 14 *beetle-brows:* overhanging brows – of the mask.

P. 48 l. 18 *rushes:* Floors at this time were commonly carpeted with rushes.

P. 48 l. 19 *grandsire phrase:* an old proverb.

P. 48 l. 20 *candle-holder:* A candle-holder holds the light whilst others work.

P. 48 ll. 22-4 *dun's the mouse . . . mire:* Mercutio must pun. Romeo's 'done' prompts him to cap it with the proverb. 'Dun' is mouse-colour, and the phrase seems to mean 'still as a mouse, as the constable says'. *Dun . . . mire:* an old winter game, called 'Dun's in the mire' in which the players haul at a heavy log, which represents the old horse stuck in the mud.

P. 48 l. 25 *save your reverence:* often contracted to 'Sir-reverence' – an apology for an improper remark or word.

P. 48 l. 31 *fine wits:* perhaps a misprint for *five wits*=the five senses, being common sense, imagination, fantasy, estimation, memory. As in Elizabethan times 'v' was written 'u' misprints between 'u' and 'n' are very common.

P. 49 l. 8 *Queen Mab:* a name for the Fairy Queen. There is an elaborate description of her in Michael Drayton's *Nymphidia: the Court of Faery*, which owes not a little to this passage.

> Hence Oberon him sport to make,
> (Their rest when weary mortals take)
> And none but only Fairies wake,
>   Descendeth for his pleasure.
> And Mab his merry Queen by night
> Bestrides young folks that lie upright
> (In elder times the Mare that hight)
>   Which plagues them out of measure.

Quartos and Folio print Mercutio's speech in prose.

atomies: little beings. The First Quarto spells 'Atomi'   P. 49 L. 12
the Second Quarto 'ottamies'; the Folio 'Atomies'.

worm . . . maid: the reading of the First Quarto; both   P. 49 LL. 20–1
Second Quarto and Folio read 'man'. Worms are said
to breed in idle fingers.

smelling out a suit: 'suit' means both 'fine clothes' and   P. 50 L. 1
a 'petition' – usually for a favour. The pun is not
uncommon. Once Sir Roger Williams appeared
before Queen Elizabeth to present a petition wearing
untanned boots. 'Poh, Williams, how your boots
stink,' said the Queen. To which he replied 'Tut,
Madam, it is my suit that stinks, not my boots.'
[Quoted in *The Sayings of Queen Elizabeth* by F.
Chamberlin.]

bakes the elf-locks: mats into knots uncombed hair.   P. 50 L. 13

sail: the reading of the First Quarto; the other texts   P. 51 L. 7
read 'suit'.

I. 5: Modern editors, disturbed by the primitive de-   P. 51 L. 11
vice of 'marching about the stage' to denote their
walking through the streets bring the scene to an end
with 'strike drum'. In the early texts there was no
division into Acts or Scenes. Modern editors by adding the divisions have not improved the text.

marchpane: cake made of almond paste, marzipan.   P. 51 L. 20

walk about: dance a measure; see Note on p., 47 l. 20.   P. 52 L. 1

worn a visor: danced.   P. 52 L. 6

A hall, a hall: 'clear a space'.   P. 52 L. 11

turn the tables up: In the Great Hall the tables were   P. 52 L. 12
separately supported on trestles. When space was
wanted they could soon be removed.

a ward: i.e. under a guardian, and so under age.   P. 52 L. 27

goodman boy: Had Capulet been a younger man there   P. 54 L. 3
would have been bloodshed, for 'boy' was a deadly
insult.

cock-a-hoop: The phrase has caused lexicographers   P. 54 L. 7

much difficulty, because in course of time it has changed its meaning. Today to be 'cock-a-hoop' = to be boastfully triumphant. In the sixteenth century it meant 'to let the liquor flow', and so 'to become utterly reckless'. Capulet means 'you want to create a disturbance, do you?'

P. 54 L. 25   *Good pilgrim*: Romeo having started the conversation with 'shrine', they continue to 'hunt the metaphor' for the next twenty lines.

P. 55 L. 7   *by th' book*: as if you had studied the art of kissing.

P. 55 L. 17   *O dear . . . debt*: O costly (yet beloved) reckoning for my life is now at the mercy of my enemy.

P. 55 L. 21   *banquet*: not a formal dinner but the light refreshments served at a dance.

P. 57 L. 8   *dull earth . . . centre out*: *Dull earth*: my dull body; *centre*: the centre of the earth, believed to be the mathematical centre of the Universe. To Romeo Juliet is now the centre.

P. 57 L. 9   *He hides*: Editors, taking Benvolio's words 'leap'd this orchard wall' to imply scenery, sometimes add some such direction as *He climbs the wall and leaps down within it*. They then begin a new scene after the departure of Benvolio and Mercutio. The original texts do not mark any *exit* for Romeo at p. 57, l. 9 or *entry* at p. 58 l. 27, for there was no change of scene, and no wall. Romeo withdraws and hides until his friends have gone: he then comes forward alone. To make this clear I have added the two stage directions *He hides* and *Romeo comes forth*. See p. 23, *The Staging of Romeo and Juliet*.

P. 57 L. 16   *Nay I'll conjure too*: The Second Quarto and Folio give this line to Benvolio; the First Quarto to Mercutio.

P. 57 L. 20   *pronounce*: the First Quarto reading; the Second Quarto reads 'provaunt', the Folio 'provant'.

P. 57 L. 23   *Young Abraham Cupid he that shot so true*: This is a much disputed line. First and Second Quartos read 'Young Abraham: Cupid he that etc.'; the Folio reads 'Abraham Cupid'. Many editors emend to 'Adam Cupid', on the ground that 'Adam' was a name given to good archers after Adam Bell, a famous archer. If Abraham is correct, then the allusion cannot yet be explained.

et cetera: a nice substitute for a nasty word. This is P. 58 L. 18
the First Quarto reading, the Second Quarto and Folio omit it.

poperin pear: another 'et cetera', literally a pear from P. 58 L. 18
Poperinghe in Flanders.

tassel-gentle: male peregrine falcon. P. 64 L. 11

Bondage is hoarse: i.e. being under the control of my P. 64 L. 12
parents, I can only whisper.

My niece: This is the reading both of Second P. 64 L. 20
Quarto and Folio, however much one would prefer to substitute 'dear' or 'sweet'. *Niece:* any close relation.

pin: centre of the target, the 'bull's eye' being a clout P. 69 L. 19
fastened by a pin.

Tybalt ... Prince of Cats: Tibalt was a traditional P. 69 L. 23
name for a fairy tale Prince of Cats.

captain of compliments: a master of perfect behaviour. P. 69 L. 24

pricksong: the melody accompanying a simple theme. P. 69 L. 25

butcher of a silk button: An expert fencer would under- P. 69 L. 27
take to touch his opponent on any button of his doublet. The rapier as a duelling weapon was newly fashionable and superseding the old long-sword, hence Mercutio's contempt for Tybalt and his fencing jargon.

first house: first school. P. 69 L. 28

first ... cause: the reasons which caused a gentleman P. 69 LL. 28-9
to issue a challenge. Touchstone (*As You Like It*, V. iv) is very eloquent on these niceties.

P. 69 LL. 29–30 *passado*, ... *hay*: *passado*: a foot movement; *punto reverso*: a backhanded stroke; *hay*: a thrust home.

P. 70 LL. 1–2 *fantasies*: fantastical fellows.

P. 70 L. 6 *pardon-mes*: i.e. *pardonnez-mois*, for your fashionable gallant must lard his discourse with foreign phrases.

P. 70 L. 13 *Laura*: Petrarch's lady to whom he wrote his love poetry.

P. 70 LL. 14–16 *Dido ... Thisbe*: These are all the tragic beauties of literary legend. Compared with Romeo's love, says Mercutio, they are, of course, but plain sluts.

P. 70 L. 15 *hildings*: worthless creatures.

P. 70 L. 16 *grey*: In Shakespeare's time the word implied a blue colour. Bacon in his essay *Of Gardens* speaks of '*crocus vernus*, both the yellow and the grey'.

P. 70 L. 18 *French slop*: baggy breeches.

P. 70 LL. 20–2 *counterfeit ... slip*: A 'slip' was a counterfeit coin or a counter; plays on these two words are common. In all ages, smart young men pass through a stage when they indulge in word-play, wit and repartee, which quickly changes its mode and fashion. Shakespeare here reproduces the fashionable wit of his generation, quick, subtle, and often bawdy, with every phrase bearing two or three meanings.

P. 71 L. 1 *pump well flower'd*: shoe punched (*pinked*) with a pattern of flowers.

P. 71 L. 10 *Switch and spurs*: i.e. at full gallop.

P. 71 LL. 10–11 *cry a match*: claim the wager.

P. 71 L. 12 *wild-goose chase*: a race where the second horseman must follow the first wherever he goes.

P. 71 L. 14 *wits ... five*: See Note on p. 48, l. 31.

P. 71 L. 20 *bitter sweeting*: a species of apple.

P. 71 L. 23 *cheveril*: kid-leather, which stretches easily.

P. 71 L. 28 *sociable*: i.e., Romeo, to Mercutio's delight, has thrown off his earlier melancholy and has become quite gay.

against the hair: against the natural inclination, as P. 72 LL. 1–2
when one strokes a cat in the wrong direction.

confidence: for conference. The Nurse's misuse of long P. 72 L. 32
words is mocked by Benvolio's *indite* (for invite).

flirt gills: 'flirting Gillian', 'tart'. P. 73 L. 25

skains mates: gangsters. P. 73 LL. 25–6

tackled stair: rope ladder, as on a sailing ship, leading P. 74 L. 26
from deck to mast.

topgallant: the small mast fixed to the top of the P. 74 L. 27
mainmast.

Two . . . away: i.e. two can keep a secret when only P. 75 L. 2
one knows it.

lay knife aboard: i.e. would have her for himself. P. 75 L. 6

A mocker that's the dog's name, . . . letter: This is the P. 75 LL. 13–14
usual emendation of a corrupt passage. It is omitted
in the First Quarto; the Second Quarto reads 'A
mocker that's the dog, name *R*. is for the no, I know
it begins with some other letter.' The Folio reads 'A
mocker that's the dog's name. *R*. is for the no, I know
it begins with some other letter.' *Dog's name, R*:
'R', wrote Ben Jonson in his English Grammar, 'is
the dog's letter, and hirreth in the sound.'

sententious: for *sentences*: clever sayings. P. 75 L. 15

bandy: a word from tennis, to hit the ball back. P. 76 L. 7

jaunce: a prancing up and down, like a restless horse. P. 76 L. 21

marry come up: an exclamation of indignation. P. 77 L. 26

blazon: describe (literally, set forth in heraldic paint- P. 79 L. 13
ing).

tutor . . . from: instruct me how to avoid. P. 80 L. 26

fee-simple: a legal phrase implying absolute posses- P. 80 L. 29
sion.

consortest: art companion of – but Mercutio takes up P. 81 L. 11
the other meaning of *consort*: a party of musicians,
playing different instruments.

P. 81 LL. 24–6 *man . . . livery:* a gentleman's 'man' wore his master's livery and followed him in public.

P. 82 L. 3 *Boy:* see Note on p. 54, l. 3.

P. 82 L. 11 *Alla stoccata carries it away: stoccata* is a thrust in fencing. Mercutio supposes that Romeo is afraid of Tybalt's superiority as a fencer.

P. 82 L. 15 *dry-beat:* beat with a stick, which does not draw blood.

P. 82 L. 17 *pilcher:* scabbard; literally, leather coat.

P. 82 L. 27 *Tybalt . . . and flies:* This, as indicated, is the First Quarto stage-direction. The Second Quarto tersely but effectively notes '*Away Tybalt*'.

P. 83 LL. 9–10 *fights by the book of arithmetic:* learns his fencing from the movements in the text book.

P. 48 L. 2 *respective lenity:* considerate mercy.

P. 84 l. 17 *fortune's fool:* fooled by fortune.

P. 86 L. 13 *interest in:* i.e. because Mercutio was my kinsman.

P. 86 L. 20 *hour:* two syllables, sometimes spelt 'hower' in Elizabethan books.

P. 86 L. 27 *Phaethon:* According to the myth, he was the son of the Sun and attempted to drive his father's chariot, but lost control of the horses.

P. 87 L. 10 *Hood . . . baiting:* images from training a wild hawk; *hood:* blindfold; *unmann'd:* untrained, wild; *baiting:* beating the wings.

P. 88 L. 15 *bare vowel ay:* See note on p. 45, ll. 20–1.

P. 88 L. 16 *cockatrice:* a fabulous creature, hatched by a serpent from a cock's egg, so dangerous that it could kill by a look.

P. 94 L. 1 *dispute:* discuss – a word implying 'hold an academic argument'.

P. 95 L. 8 *deep an O:* such loud lamentation.

P. 96 LL. 24–5 *powder . . . set a-fire:* Elizabethan firearms were set off by applying a lighted match (or fuse). As the match was kept constantly alight, accidents were easy.

dismember'd . . . defence: blown to pieces by your own   P. 96 L. 26
weapon.

watch be set: The watch went on duty each evening.   P. 97 L. 30

reflex of Cynthia's brow: reflection of the moon.   P. 100 L. 9

lark . . . change eyes: The toad has beautiful eyes, but   P. 100 L. 20
a harsh croak, whilst the lark's eyes are ugly.

hunts-up: song sung or played to arouse the hunters   P. 100 L. 23
early in the morning.

Dry sorrow drinks our blood: Sighing was believed to   P. 101 L. 20
consume the heart's blood, so sorrow dries the colour
from Juliet's face.

She goeth down . . . : See *The Staging of Romeo and Ju-*   P. 101 L. 27
liet, p. 25.

conduit: a fountain, often in the shape of a human   P. 104 L. 11
figure.

chop-logic: one who answers back argumentatively.   P. 104 L. 32

green-sickness: a malady most incident to maids.   P. 105 L. 7

her fortune's tender: when good fortune is offered her.   P. 106 L. 10

all . . . nothing: there isn't a chance.   P. 107 L. 11

label: the strip of parchment by which the seal is   P. 110 L. 14
attached to a document.

charnel-house: It was a custom in Shakespeare's time   P. 111 L. 6
for the bones of the dead, after they had lain in the
earth for a time, to be taken up and pitched into a
charnel-house – a custom which Shakespeare seems
to have abhorred, as can be seen from the grave-dig-
gers' scene in *Hamlet* [V. 1].

inconstant toy: fickle fancy.   P. 112 L. 14

Farewell, God knows: See Introduction p. 15 for the   P. 115 L. 12
original source of this soliloquy.

mandrakes: A forked root, narcotically poisonous,   P. 116 L. 12
often fantastically shaped like a human body. Various
legends were told about it, as that it uttered shrieks
when uprooted which would drive a man mad.

P. 116 L. 24   *She falls upon her bed within the curtains*: See p. 25.

P. 116 L. 29   *Pastry*: one of the rooms in the kitchen department of a Great House.

P. 117 L. 6   *cot-quean*: literally, a labourer's wife; but here, a man who meddles in household matters which do not concern him.

P. 118 L. 4   *IV. 5*: This scene division has been mistakenly inserted by editors, for the Nurse does not leave the stage. See p. 26.

P. 118 L. 11   *set up his rest*: A metaphor from *primero*, a card game, where the phrase meant to hold one's hand: hence to make up the mind or be determined.

P. 120 L. 17   *confusion's care*: 'The way to take care of confusion is not to make more confusion.' 'Care' is, however, often emended to 'cure'.

P. 120 L. 32   *rosemary*: Rosemary was used both for weddings and funerals. Thus Thomas Dekker (in *The Wonderful Year*, 1603) tells the story of a bride who died of the plague on her wedding day: 'Here is a strange alteration, for the rosemary that was washed in sweet water to set out the bridal is now wet in tears to furnish her burial.'

P. 121 L. 4   *nature's . . . merriment*: the reasonable man laughs at grief because the dead has gone to a better place.

P. 121 L. 26   *Enter Peter*: The Second Quarto read *Enter Will Kemp* – the famous Clown of the Lord Chamberlain's Company, who took the part.

P. 122 L. 12   *note us*: in the double sense of 'obscure' and 'make musical notes on'.

P. 123 L. 19   ⟨*booted*⟩: thereby indicating that he has ridden far.

P. 124 L. 2   *deny you stars*: usually emended to 'defy'; but 'deny' (will thwart) is good sense. Romeo has been star-crossed throughout; now he denies to Fate the power to do him any worse injury.

searchers of the town ... infectious pestilence ... Seal'd P. 126 LL.
up the doors: Although Shakespeare took the incident 19–21
from Brooke's poem, it would have reminded his
audience vividly of the horrors of plague in London
a few months before. In 1592 and 1593 there was a
particularly bad outbreak, and many regulations were
then made. Amongst others, it was ordered that in
every house infected 'the whole family and residents
therein at the time of such infection shall remain con-
tinually without departing out of the same, and with
the doors and windows of the hall, shop, or other
nether part of the house shut by the space of 28 days.'
Further, 'for every parish there shall be appointed
two sober ancient women to be sworn to be viewers
of the bodies of such as shall die in time of infection,
and two other to be viewers of such as shall be sick
and suspected of infection.' [*Shakespeare Association
Facsimiles,* No. 7, edited by W. P. Barrett, pp. ix, xi.]

villainous shame: Paris suspects that Romeo wishes to P. 129 L. 13
steal some part of the dead bodies from the tomb of
the Montagues to work spells against them by necro-
mancy.

a lantern: i.e. the top of a dome or tower. P. 130 L. 16

For fear of that I still will stay with thee: The conclud- P. 131 L. 6
ing lines of this speech were rewritten. They appear
in the Second Quarto thus: –

> And never from this pallat of dym night.
> Depart againe, come lye thou in my arme,
> Heer's to thy health, where ere thou tumblest in.
> O true Appothecarie!
> Thy drugs are quicke. Thus with a kisse I die.
> Depart againe, here, here, will I remaine,
> With wormes that are thy Chamber-maides: O
>   here
> Will I set up my everlasting rest: ...

The speech continues as in the text ending: –

> The dashing Rocks, thy seasick weary barke:
> Heeres to my Love. O true Appothecary
> Thy drugs are quicke. Thus with a kisse I die.

Here both original and revised version remain. In later quartos the repeated lines were omitted.

There are other traces of revision, or different strata of composition in the play. The first scene, for instance, between Friar Laurence and Romeo (pp. 65–8) is written all in rhyme in a metre altogether stiffer than the later passage in III. 3 (pp. 91–8).

P. 131 L. 15   *dateless ... death:* an everlasting agreement with death that buys up wholesale.

P. 135 L. 12   *Seal up ... outrage:* Here the curtains are closed concealing the three bodies. *Outrage:* violent deeds.

P. 135 L. 15   *general of your woes:* leader of your lamentations.

GLOSSARY

a' : he
advanc'd : promoted
all along : at full length
ambling : elaborate walking
amerce : punish
and : if
antic face : grotesque mask
apace : quickly
aqua vitae : liquor, spirits
aspired : ascended to
associate : accompany
Aurora : the dawn

bankrout : bankrupt
behoveful : suitable
bent : intention
berlady : by Our Lady
bescreen'd : concealed
beshrew : bad luck to
blaze : make public
bosom's Lord : heart
bower : embower
buckler : small shield used with
  the long sword
by rote : by heart

caitiff : wretch
canker : maggot
canker'd : corrupted

chapless : without cheeks
charge : importance
checkring : variegating
chinks : cash
circumstance : knowledge of the
  facts
coil : confusion, fuss
commission : authority
conceit : imagination
consorted : allied
contract : bethrothal
cop'st : encounterest
count : reckoning
countervail : counterbalance
County : Count
crow : crowbar
crowkeeper : bird-scarer
cull'd : collected

deny : repudiate
discover : reveal
dislike : displease
division : melody, harmony
doublet : short coat
dump : doleful ditty

ensign : flag

fantasy : fancy
fay : faith
fearful : full of fear
fettle : make ready

fleckled: dappled
fleer: mock
fond: foolishly affectionate
frank: generous
full of charge: important directions
fume: mist

ghostly: spiritual
gleek: mocking retort
God shield: God prevent
green: fresh

hare: prostitute
harlotry: silly girl
hilding: worthless creature
humour: (1) whim, (2) moisture
humorous: whimsical

indite: for invite

lace: cover with a pattern
lady-bird: sweetheart
level: aim
limits: boundaries

mammet: doll
manage: conduct
maw: stomach
measure: formal dance
mew'd: caged
mickle: mighty
minion: hussy
modern: commonplace
mouse-hunt: wencher

move: discuss with
muffled: blindfold

natural: fool
needly: needfully
nice: trifling
nimble-pinioned: quick winged.

o'erperch: fly over
orisons: prayers
osier cage: wicker basket
owes: owns

passed: surpassed
passing: exceedingly
Phoebus: the sun
pitch: top of the flight of a hawk
pois'd: weighed
poor John: dried hake
portly: worthy
presently: immediately
pressed: weighed down
prick: point
princox: saucy boy
prodigious: ominous
prolixity: tedious excess

quit: reward

reeking: stinking
ropery: roguery
runagate: runaway
rushed: brushed

sadness: seriousness
season: keep fresh with salt
shield: forbid

shrift : sacramental absolution following confession
smatter : prattle
sorted : chosen
sounded : swooned
sped : done for
spinner : spider
spleen : anger
stakes : fastens down
steads : benefits
still : always
stinted : stopped
stratagems : violent deeds
stuffed : full

teen : grief
tempering : allaying
tender : offer
tetchy : peevish
thought long : long desired

timeless : everlasting, untimely
Titan : the sun
toy : trifle

uneven : indirect, unusual
unfurnished : unprovided
untainted : unbiassed
unthrifty : unlucky

validity : worth
vanished : escaped from
versal : universal
vestal : virgin

wanton : spoilt child
ward : minor, needing a guardian
washing : swashing, sweeping

'zounds : by God's wounds

THE STORY OF PENGUIN CLASSICS

Before 1946 ... 'Classics' are mainly the domain of academics and students, without readable editions for everyone else. This all changes when a little-known classicist, E. V. Rieu, presents Penguin founder Allen Lane with the translation of Homer's *Odyssey* that he has been working on and reading to his wife Nelly in his spare time.

1946 *The Odyssey* becomes the first Penguin Classic published, and promptly sells three million copies. Suddenly, classic books are no longer for the privileged few.

1950s Rieu, now series editor, turns to professional writers for the best modern, readable translations, including Dorothy L. Sayers's *Inferno* and Robert Graves's *The Twelve Caesars*, which revives the salacious original.

1960s 1961 sees the arrival of the Penguin Modern Classics, showcasing the best twentieth-century writers from around the world. Rieu retires in 1964, hailing the Penguin Classics list as 'the greatest educative force of the 20th century'.

1970s A new generation of translators arrives to swell the Penguin Classics ranks, and the list grows to encompass more philosophy, religion, science, history and politics.

1980s The Penguin American Library joins the Classics stable, with titles such as *The Last of the Mohicans* safeguarded. Penguin Classics now offers the most comprehensive library of world literature available.

1990s Penguin Popular Classics are launched, offering readers budget editions of the greatest works of literature. Penguin Audiobooks brings the classics to a listening audience for the first time, and in 1999 the launch of the Penguin Classics website takes them online to an ever larger global readership.

The 21st Century Penguin Classics are rejacketed for the first time in nearly twenty years. This world famous series now consists of more than 1,300 titles, making the widest range of the best books ever written available to millions – and constantly redefining the meaning of what makes a 'classic'.

The Odyssey continues ...

The best books ever written